AN AVIATOR AT HEART

ILYAN KEI LAVANWAY

Ilyan Kei Lavanway
Cocoa, Florida
USA

AN AVIATOR AT HEART
Copyright © 2014 Ilyan Kei Lavanway
Cover design by Ilyan Kei Lavanway
Illustrated by Ilyan Kei Lavanway
All rights reserved.

No part of this book may be reproduced in any form whatsoever, whether by graphic, visual, electronic, film, microfilm, tape recording, or any other means, without prior written permission of the author, except in the case of brief passages embodied in reviews and articles.

ISBN-13: 978-0-9768004-9-1
ISBN-10: 0-9768004-9-7

Published by Ilyan Kei Lavanway
Cocoa, Florida, USA

Library of Congress Control Number: 2013923059

Dedicated to my Dad.

Disclaimer

Why a disclaimer? Because, sadly, that's the world we live in, these days. Flight procedures described in this book are expressed largely from memory, two to three decades after the fact. Some are not recommended. Do not substitute any procedures described herein for current operating practices. Refer to official documentation and procedures before operating any aircraft.

So, now do you feel like you are about to read an aviation version of Fast and Furious? Sorry, the main character in this story is not as handsome as Paul Walker and cannot kick butt like Vin Diesel, but I think you will still enjoy the story.

Contents

Acknowledgments v
Preface vii
Chapter One 1
Chapter Two 9
Chapter Three 11
Chapter Four 15
Chapter Five 27
Chapter Six 29
Chapter Seven 39
Chapter Eight 47
Chapter Nine 51
Chapter Ten 59
Chapter Eleven 67
Chapter Twelve 71
Chapter Thirteen 75
Chapter Fourteen 79
Chapter Fifteen 83

Chapter Sixteen	97
Chapter Seventeen	103
Chapter Eighteen	107
Chapter Nineteen	111
Chapter Twenty	115
Chapter Twenty-One	119
Chapter Twenty-Two	121
Chapter Twenty-Three	125
Chapter Twenty-Four	133
Chapter Twenty-Five	135
Chapter Twenty-Six	139
Chapter Twenty-Seven	141
Chapter Twenty-Eight	165
Chapter Twenty-Nine	171
Chapter Thirty	177
Chapter Thirty-One	181
Postface	183
Aircraft Flown	185
Sketches	187
Photos	219

ACKNOWLEDGMENTS

The photographs of the aircraft and cockpit featured on the front and back covers of this book, respectively, were taken by David Greene. They can be found on the internet at: http://www2.airliners.net/photo/Piper-PA-28R-200-Cherokee/0249778/L/

Please forgive any misspelled names. Going from memory and handwritten records after nearly thirty years presents a spelling challenge with a few of the names.

The following alphabetical list is by no means exhaustive. These are but a few of the individuals who touched the life of a young Aviator, and to whom his deepest gratitude is extended forever:

Allen Johnson
Bill Saul
Cherene (Freenie) Clark
Chris Fredericks
Daling Family
Danny and Kathy Fielding
Dawn Lambert
Gary Moses

Gary W. Giffar
Gerhard Ellestad
Homer and Jean Longhurst
Hunter Moses
James Follansbee
James (Jim) Watson
Jay Farrell
John D. Kell
Jule Ellestad
Larry Longhurst
Mark and Sue (Nora) Norris
Matt Langston
Melissa Delvecchio
Merle and Elsie Jacobsen
Mike
Miss Cole
Mr. Babcock
Mr. Bradley
Mr. Jaspers
Patrick Kendall
Robert (Bob) Meinke
Roxanne Clay
Stan (Seattle-based Boeing engineer)
Timothy (Tim) Johnson
Tony Riffe
Wally Olson
Willard Skoglun

PREFACE

The story you are about to read is true. The places and people mentioned in this story exist. The names have not been altered, nor should they need to be, as there is much good to be said of them. The events described in this story happened. The dialogue expressed herein was actually spoken, or is typical of what would have been said in the given situation.

The events described herein are not necessarily presented in chronological order. There is some jumping back and forth for the sake of background and emphasis, and just to keep things interesting. This story is not an exhaustive account. It contains a few highlights of a period of youth.

You live in a different world than the one in which this story took place. This story happened before there were any such things as GoPro video cameras, YouTube, Facebook, Twitter, MySpace, or whatever other personal recording devices and connectivity interfaces have entrenched themselves in your everyday life.

Many people have done far greater and more astonishing and noteworthy things than what you will read about here. Nevertheless, you can get something worthwhile out of this story.

Much of what was once impressive is now commonplace and unimpressive. So, rewind your paradigm and step back in time. Written in retrospect some twenty to thirty years after the fact, this story will allow you to benefit from the insights of hindsight while being thoroughly entertained.

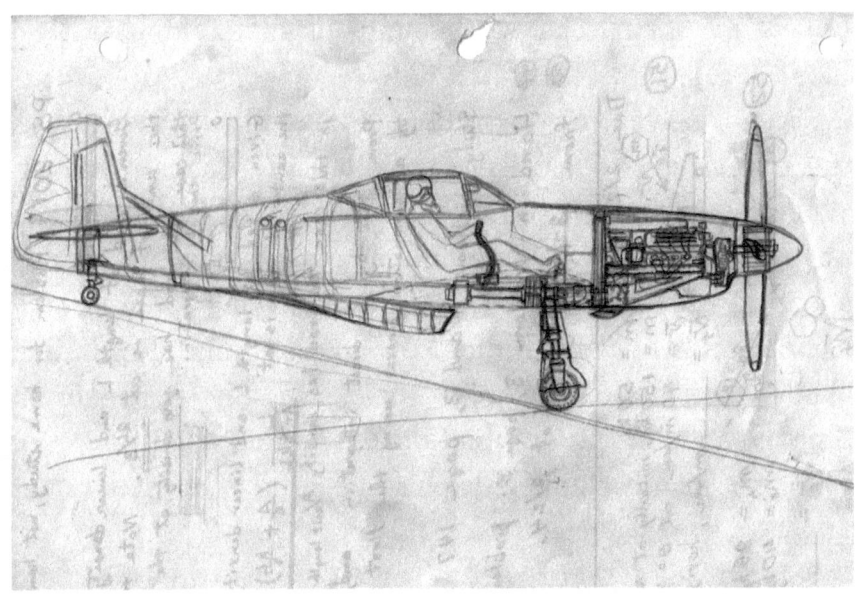

Chapter One

Nice guys almost always finish last. And they almost never get the girl. Do you want to know why nice guys usually finish last and seldom get the girl? I'll tell you anyway. It's because nice guys are afraid to take risks with people's hearts, especially their own. It's one of the most ironic manifestations of pride ever to disgrace the human race. While trying to avoid rejection, nice guys end up being the ones rejecting or neglecting the girl. Not very nice, is it?

In fact, it's bogus. That stuff sounds like something out of a movie. Probably is, but it fits.

For all his yearning to be the quintessential chick magnet, the young Aviator felt like a walking can of babe repellent. Whenever he would enter a room full of pretty girls, he made an impression akin to a lightbulb in a roach motel. Of course, sneezing at a Church youth dance and blowing a Maraschino Cherry out his nose and then showing it around exclaiming, "Look what shot out my nose!" or passing the sacrament on Sunday and, albeit unintentionally, letting fly a burst of flatulence like a ripping sheet as he rounded a pew might factor in, somewhere. Just a smidge.

Surprisingly, there were other occasions when he could have had any girl he wanted. There's a lot more to this story than can fit in one book, but we'll get to the part where the nice guy gets really stupid and doesn't get the girl. Or does he?

The price of omission is often worse than the price of commission. Better to risk offense and do something, anything, even if it's inappropriate or against the rules, than to do nothing and wallow in cowardice, regretfully wondering what might have been. You are one of three things: hot, cold, or lukewarm. Take your pick. One of them is equivalent to vomit. It says so right there in the Bible.

The eldest of eight siblings, seven living, the young Aviator was born in Ellensburg, Washington in 1967. He grew up in Wenatchee, Washington, and spent his senior year of high school in Waterville, Washington. Wheat country. During his summers in high school and college, he drove wheat tucks and combines. That was fun work. He loved it.

Throughout his youth, the young Aviator was extremely shy, pathetically shy. Perhaps even pathologically shy. He was a tall, well-built, serious, geeky, eyebrow plucking, trichotillomaniacal nerd who consistently donned out-of-style, second hand attire and wore thick eyeglasses as wide as plates.

At age seven, temporarily living in Missouri while his Dad, Victor Gordon LaVanway, attended a couple of years of chiropractic school, the young Aviator was already asking how airplanes fly and how to pilot one. When his Dad, who was also a private pilot, explained it to him, the young Aviator understood everything his Dad described.

Dad explained Bernoulli's principle and how it contributes to aerodynamic lift on an airplane wing. Dad also gave him a pilot handbook that explained the different flight instruments. Dad gave him an old, pocket size, aluminum E6-B flight computer in a leather sheath. The Aviator used that E6-B on nearly every cross country flight he made. He still has it. It's stowed in a box somewhere at home, awaiting resurrection.

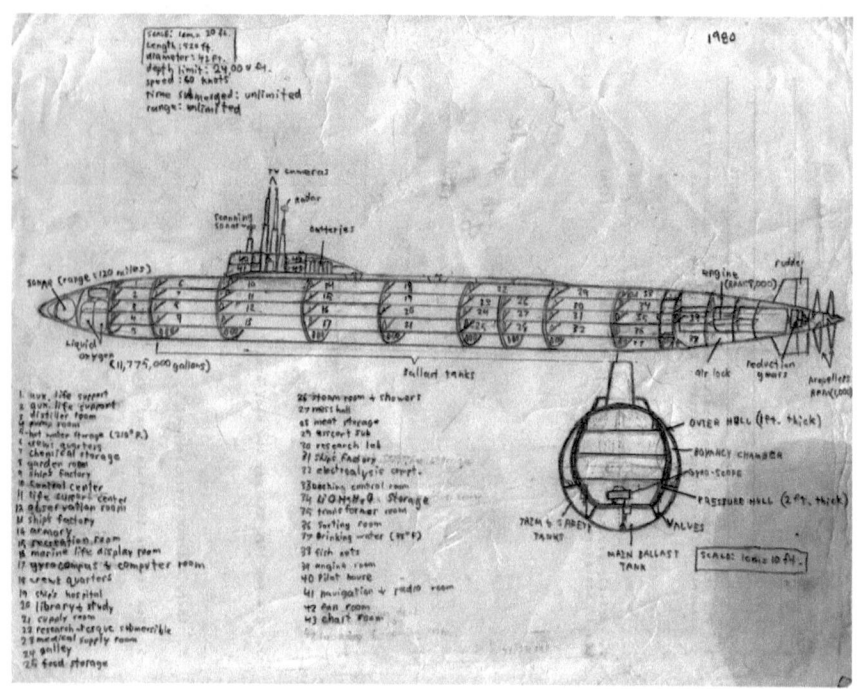

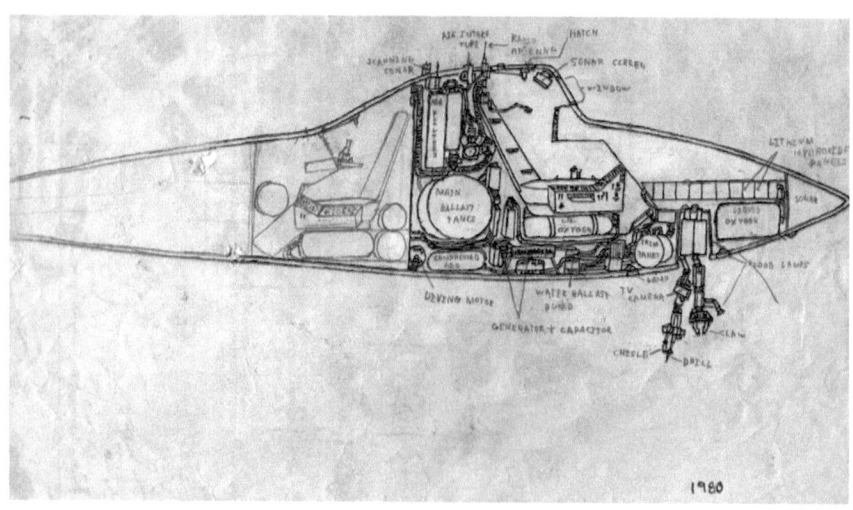

From age seven to age twelve, the young Aviator developed intense interests in subjects ranging from paleontology to marine biology to submarines. His interest in submarines almost caused him to fail Mr. Jasper's seventh grade drafting class. The young Aviator insisted on drawing cutaway views of his own conceptual submarines rather than drawing the assigned circles and squares and triangles. At one point, Mr. Jaspers told him, "You're really sucking swamp water for somebody of your ability!"

The young Aviator continued his academic free fall to the point of nearly dropping out of school in eighth grade. He wanted to go with his Grandpa, Lovell LaVanway, to live in the jungles of the Yucatan Peninsula. Grandpa was his hero, a survivor, a renegade, and a mechanical genius. Grandpa was once a private pilot, too.

Grandpa wasn't perfect by any stretch of the imagination. He always admitted he was "just a man." But, the young Aviator, on some level, secretly identified with the rebellious streak that ran deep in Grandpa's blood.

Grandpa spent most of his later years working on an invention he was convinced could harness the principles of magnetism to generate perpetual mechanical energy. Of course, the young Aviator immediately began imagining how such an engine could be applied to airplanes.

Grandpa did not live long enough to perfect his idea. The day will come when the concept he was exploring will be as common as the machines you take for granted in your daily life.

Grandpa made long visits to the young Aviator's home at 309 South Chelan Street in Wenatchee. Grandpa visited on two separate occasions while the young Aviator was in his early teens. Grandpa had nine children through a Mexican girl named Aurelia, while living in Mexico and Texas. They had eight sons and one daughter. The daughter's name was Candy. Fitting name. She was a sweet girl. Kind of cute, too. She went everywhere with Grandpa. The Aviator had a secret crush on her for years. She may have felt the same toward him, but nothing ever came of it.

Family dynamics were interesting, to say the least. Eight of Grandpa's Mexican kids came with him to Wenatchee. They traveled and lived in their converted school bus. Since these kids were from a different mother than the Aviator's Dad's mother, Grandpa's kids were half-uncles and half-aunt to the Aviator.

In some ways, the Aviator considered it a refreshing departure from convention to have half-uncles and a half-aunt who were younger by several years. Some were a bit older, but about half of them were as young as, or younger than the Aviator. Nobody knows exactly how old any of Grandpa's Mexican brood was. None of them had accurate birth records, at least not in the United States.

During sixth grade or seventh grade, the young Aviator came home from school one day to learn that Grandpa had left and gone back to Mexico or Texas. The young Aviator went into the bathroom and secretly wept. He had never missed anyone so much, before or since. But, let's not get ahead of ourselves.

The young Aviator joined the local Civil Air Patrol at age thirteen and planned to enter the United States Air Force as an officer. He knew he would eventually have to make a decision before the start of his ninth grade school year. Ninth grade was when academic performance began to matter on college applications.

A four-year bachelor's degree was prerequisite to becoming an officer in the U.S. military. So, from the beginning of ninth grade onward, the young Aviator set his mind to study hard and complete all his homework on time or ahead of time.

DATE 19 84	MAKE MODEL	REG. NUMBER	FROM / TO	PROCEDURES — MANEUVERS	AIRCRAFT SEL
5-10-84	C-152	48868	EAT - KENNEWIK - EAT	cross-country	2:0
5-13-84	C-172	51785	EAT - Lcl	turns, slow flight	1:1
5-19-84	C-172	48445	EAT - Lcl	takeoffs & landings, slow flight, turns	1:0
5-26-84	C-172	51785	RAT - Lcl	X-C Waterville, CF II-165 7079 James W Walton	.4
5-26-84	C-172	48445	EAT - Lcl	turns	.7
5-28-84	C-152	48868	EAT - CONNEL	cross country, takeoffs & landings, turns	1:4
5-28-84	C-152	48868	CONNEL - EAT	cross country	.9
SPECIAL ENDORSEMENTS – BIENNIAL FLIGHT REVIEW – GROUND INSTRUCTION				PAGE TOTAL	7:5
				BROUGHT FORWARD	75:9
				TOTAL	83:4

AIRCRAFT CATEGORY & CLASS		FLIGHT CONDITIONS					CROSS COUNTRY	PILOT TIME		TOTAL
SEL	MEL	DAY	NIGHT	INSTRUMENT				DUAL	P.I.C.	
				ACTUAL	HOOD	SIMULATOR				
2:0	:	2:0	:	:	:	:	2:0	:	2:0	2:0
1:1	:	1:1	:	:	:	:	:	1:1	1:1	1:1
1:0	:	1:0	:	:	:	:	:	1:0	1:0	1:0
.4	:	.4	:	:	:	:	.4	:	.4	.4
.7	:	.7	:	:	:	:	:	.7	.7	.7
1:4	:	1:4	:	:	:	:	1:4	:	1:4	1:4
.9	:	.9	:	:	:	:	.9	:	.9	.9
7:5	:	7:5	:	:	:	:	4:3	.4	7:1	7:5
75:9	:	71:0	4:9	:	4:7	:	38:4	26:8	49:1	75:9
83:4	:	78:5	4:9	:	4:7	:	42:7	27:2	56:2	83:4

Chapter Two

On one occasion, later in high school, May 10, 1984, to be exact, the young Aviator was particularly glad he had taken the initiative to complete his homework ahead of time. Because of his promptness and diligence in getting his homework done early, he succeeded in convincing his History teacher to let him cut class for the day to help a friend, Chris Fredericks, resolve a transportation scheduling discrepancy.

Chris had missed the bus to a track meet in Kennewick, Washington. That was a three-hour drive from Wenatchee. But, it was only a one-hour flight. Chris missed his bus. He didn't miss the track meet. And the coaches got something to squawk about.

"Chris, you made it! How? You missed the bus. When did you leave?" someone grilled him as he and the Aviator sauntered over to the Kennewick High School track field from the airfield a few blocks away.

"Oh, we left about and hour ago," Chris replied, smiling.

"Wow, you must've been really flying!"

"We were."

Over a decade later, the Aviator's youngest brother, Alex, who graduated from Wenatchee High School, told the Aviator that people were still talking about how the Aviator had flown Chris Fredericks to that track meet in the Tri-Cities back in the day. Someone convoluted the story through the passing of rumors to say that the Aviator had actually landed on the school's track field. That didn't happen. He did buzz the field at an extremely low altitude, however. We've jumped ahead a bit here. Rewind.

Chapter Three

During the young Aviator's ninth grade school year, some of his teachers commented on his complete and total academic turnaround. His ninth grade civics teacher was particularly impressed by his civics project. Using glue, toothpicks, and wooden surgical sticks and thread, the young Aviator built a model bridge. It was a scale replica of the old railway bridge that crossed the Columbia River between Wenatchee and East Wenatchee. The old bridge has been converted into a pedestrian bridge.

"There is one person in this class who has worked harder than anyone, and has made a complete change from last year," the civics teacher commented, pointing out the young Aviator in front of the entire class. All heads turned. The comment and the looks evoked mixed emotions in the shy, unpopular lad. Embarrassment, pride, gratitude, vindication, and perhaps a fleeting fantasy that girls might notice him. At any rate, it made the young Aviator feel appreciated.

He got nearly straight-A grades from ninth grade on through high school and into the first trimester of his freshman year of college at Embry-Riddle Aeronautical University in Prescott, Arizona. After that, life became filled with other distractions, and his grades slipped to barely passing. But again, let's not get ahead of ourselves. Her name was Kathy Hubbard, by the way. And that never worked out.

The young Aviator was no ordinary kid when he set his mind to the pursuit of subjects that fascinated him. He could not settle for a mere casual familiarity with subjects that caught his attention. He always had to try to understand the Why of everything. Knowing the What and the How was never enough.

Whatever his interest, the young Aviator attacked it with passion and determination. He had a one-tack mind. The correct terms for that trait are singleness of heart, singleness of mind, and singleness of purpose.

However, being single-minded was a double-edged sword. Anything outside the scope of his interest wasn't even worth thinking about, let alone doing. He wasn't winning any popularity contests. Nor was he always making the strides others may have thought he should make.

Styles? Fads? What a waste of thought! Sports? Who cares?! Eagle Scout? Barely squeaked that one in before the age deadline of eighteen. Community involvement? Bite me! Take initiative? Be proactive? Only if there's an airplane involved. Leadership? Yeah. That can be delegated right back upstream by default. Unless it involves aviation.

Throughout seventh and eighth grades, the young Aviator routinely skipped Physical Education (PE) class, pep rallies, and mandatory school assemblies, escaping to the school library to read about submarines and airplanes. School spirit? Ha! Shove it up your biblical donkey! When he asked the school librarian at Orchard Junior High School (middle school) to help him find a certain book on submarines, she commented, "You're still in that rut?"

From as early as age twelve onward, the young Aviator diligently studied, ate, drank, and slept aviation. It was all he thought about. Well, almost.

CHAPTER FOUR

The wet-behind-the-ears Aviator yearned to fly, but he also had an intense longing to find a girl with whom he could share his mind and heart and future adventures. At age thirteen, he was not seeking a casual girlfriend. He was definitely not interested in group dating. Group dating. What a load of crap!

He wanted to find a girl with whom he could pair off as a soul mate. He wanted a wife. That is to say, he wanted to begin courting a girl that he could make his wife when the proper time would come. He did not necessarily intend to become a thirteen-year-old husband. He knew he had manly duties to accomplish before he could marry.

However, being told he had to wait until he was fourteen years old to attend a Church dance made him wroth beyond description. He was already taking initiative beyond his years to study aviation entirely on his own, driven by his exuberant anticipation of flying airplanes. He managed his own money, what little he could earn here and there. He was serious about courtship and marriage, even at age thirteen. That, of course, was belied by his shyness.

Because of what he considered at the time to be an absurdly asinine Church standard, he was taught that it would be inappropriate to attend a Church dance prior to turning fourteen. Not that he would have suddenly overcome his shyness and actually asked a girl to dance, but the principle of the matter just irked him something fierce.

He channeled his energy all the more intensely into studying and pondering what it would be like to fly airplanes. Aviation was, after all, his first love, and the one with whom it was no sin to dance at any age.

While the Aviator was still thirteen years old, he studied everything he could about airplanes and how to fly them. He spent several hours a day listening to oldies music and visualizing everything he could imagine about what it might feel like and sound like to be at the controls of various different airplanes.

The young Aviator spent hours browsing the airplanes listed in an old magazine his Dad had kept. He compared each airplane's listed characteristics against the listed characteristics of the other airplanes. He studied and tried to visualize aircraft performance specifications, engine power ratings, aircraft gross weights, empty weights, payload capacities, fuel capacities, ranges, wingspans, wing areas, wing loading, and other such technical information.

He would ponder why an engine of a given size and horsepower on an airplane of a given size and weight and wing area would yield certain performance characteristics.

Then, he would ponder why an engine of similar size and power on a different airplane would yield different performance results. Then, he would interpolate and extrapolate to develop his own ideas, and then measure the accuracy of his own concepts against other listed airplanes having parameters similar to those of his own conceptual designs. It was an intuitive exercise. It was the best he could do with what he had.

To the young Aviator, this entire information gathering and concept synthesis process was not just to pack his brain full of gee-whiz facts and figures and mere trivia. This information served as a set of parameters from which he could construct thought experiments in preparation for future realization.

He memorized pictures of different airplanes in as much detail as he could find. He coupled the imagery with the technical specifications and then daydreamed for hours at a stretch, in deep thought simulations, trying to imagine every sound, every sensation of movement, every control pressure in different flight conditions, and how the view might look from the cockpit. He also visualized how he might appear from an observer's perspective.

His young mind became his own flight simulator for aircraft he had never even seen in real life. He did this for many types of airplanes, from the big, four-engine Douglas DC-7 and Lockheed Constellation to the North American P-51 Mustang to the small, two-seat Cessna-152 that would soon become his first cockpit experience.

He knew he would only be able to afford to start flying lessons in a two-seat Cessna-152, so he studied everything he could about that airplane before even sitting in one. He stared at cockpit photos, browsed performance specifications, and pondered photos of the airplane in flight. He imagined the airspeeds appropriate for various flight conditions and what the slipstream might sound like at different airspeeds. He imagined the sound of the engine at different power settings. He imagined the feel of the yoke in his hand and the control pressures he thought he might encounter during takeoff, climbs, turns, descents, and landings.

The too-young-to-go-to-a-church-dance issue came up when the Aviator was still thirteen years old. He was drooling over a seventeen-year-old girl, Dawn Lambert, whom he had met at The Church of Jesus Christ of Latter-day Saints in East Wenatchee.

Dawn had recently been baptized and had shared a beautiful testimony during sacrament meeting one Sunday. The Aviator was smitten. She was the one, he thought. She seemed deeply spiritual. She was also quite pretty. And she was going to be at the upcoming Church youth dance. He wanted to go to the dance just to see her.

He prayed every day about whether or not she would be the girl he should eventually marry. He did not intend to marry her immediately, of course. He simply wanted to begin a long courtship that would lead to marriage in the years that would follow. God seemed to be dropping hints, but the Aviator didn't catch a clue.

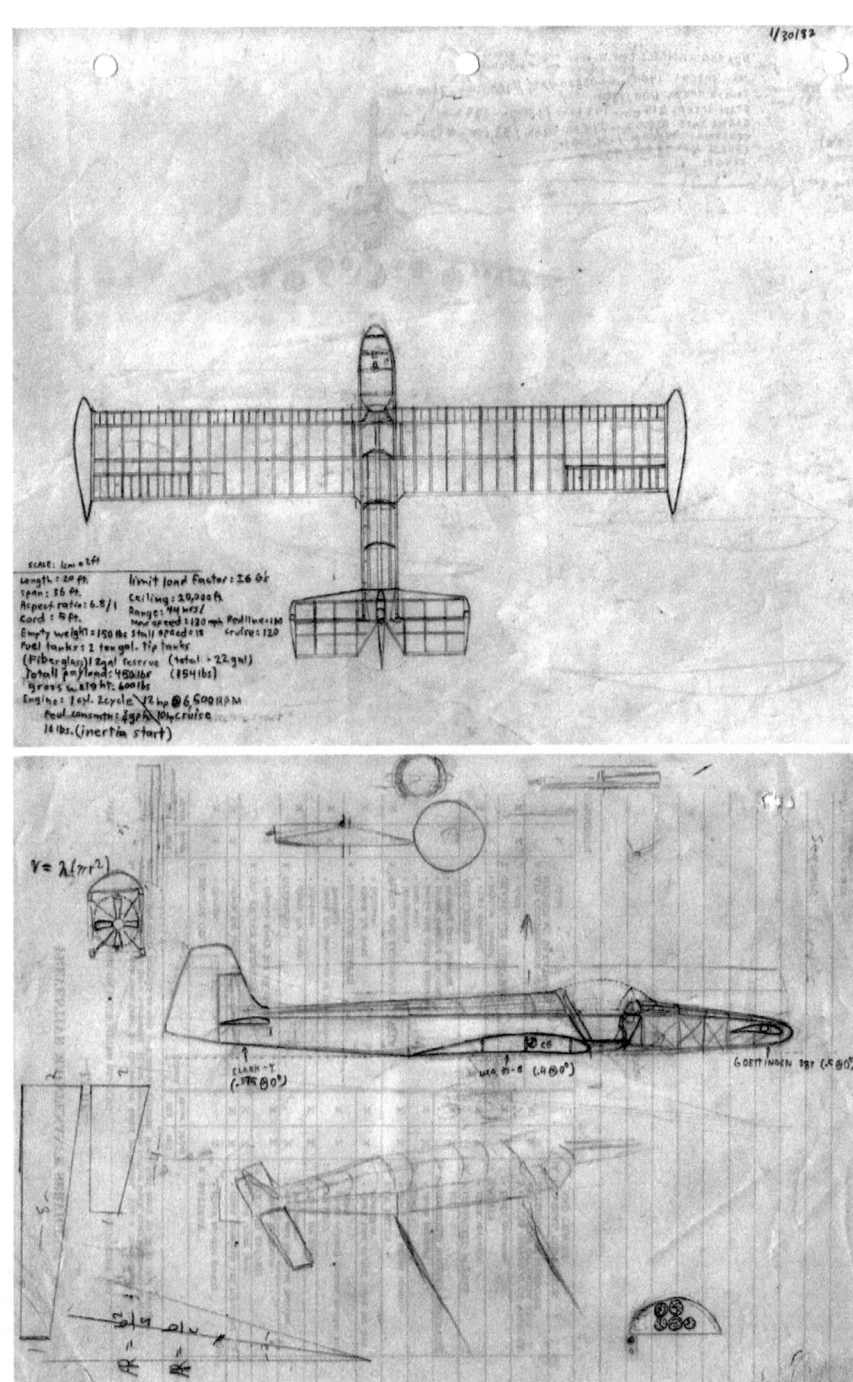

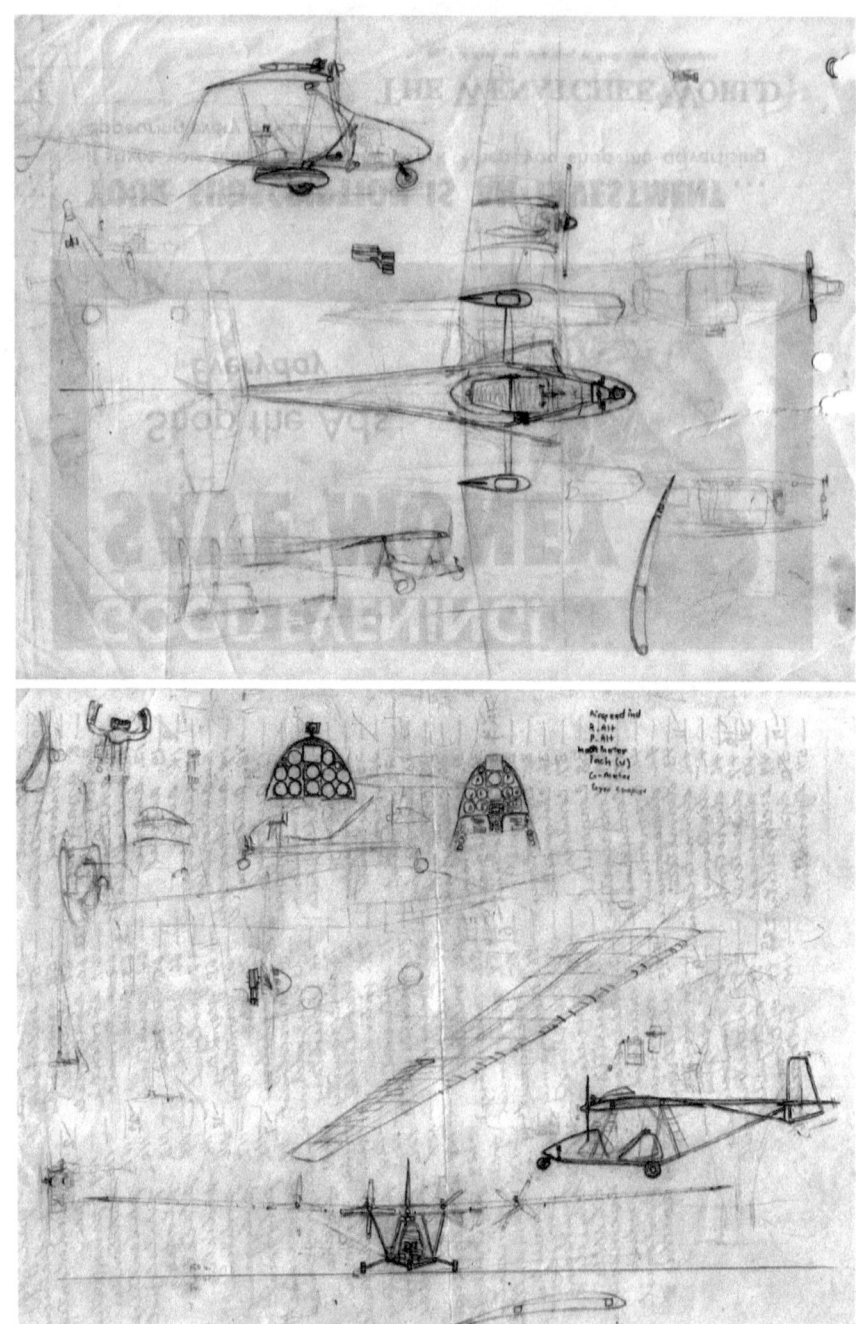

The young Aviator often spent hours sketching aircraft he thought he could build if only he had the right tools and materials. He would listen to 1950s music and nostalgic country music on a mono cassette tape player and a radio in the study his Dad had installed in the house on South Chelan Street. The sweet strains of Patsy Cline, Loretta Lynn, Hank Williams Senior, Merle Haggard, Elvis Presley, Buddy Holly and many others of similar genres put him in the zone.

Music often evoked strong emotions within his heart, and catalyzed vivid, dynamic imaginations in his mind. Dawn Lambert was frequently featured in his fanciful flights and the adventures upon which he embarked within his mind as he mentally test piloted the airplane designs he was sketching. His Mom once told him he could not woo a girl with an airplane.

Mom was probably right. But, flying airplanes was the only thing the young Aviator knew he could be good at even before he did it. He secretly felt aviation was his edge. At the time, he would have never admitted he was into maintaining any kind of an edge. But, he was.

Nobody among his peers seemed interested in aviation, so he had little or no competition. In his world, a teenage pilot was a prodigy. Surely that would impress the girls. So, why not woo a girl with an airplane? Other guys used football and cars and stylish clothes, and that seemed to work well for them. The young Aviator could offer something the other guys could not. Bear in mind that back in the day, aviation was romantic and masculine, as well as technical and adventurous. Perhaps not so, now. At least not in the eyes of the world. Too many girls in the cockpits these days.

The Aviator was both a hopeless romantic and a technically minded stallion of fierce determination. Even in his youth, his Mom often described him as a man of steel and velvet. He never did read that book. Maybe someday he will.

The young Aviator had his own kind of synergy going on between his mind and his heart. He would often get embarrassed if anyone caught him listening to music. There was nothing to be embarrassed about. He just didn't want anyone interfering with the flow of his thoughts or eavesdropping on his anachronistic taste in tunes.

The young Aviator fasted and prayed often over the course of several months to know if Dawn Lambert would be the girl he should marry in due time, after he would complete two years as a full time missionary. He knew it was his duty to serve a full time mission, and he had no intention of marrying until after he had fulfilled his duty. He simply wanted to know ahead of time who he was going to marry when he would return from missionary service. After all, we're talking about eternity, here. He even asked for his patriarchal blessing in the hopes that God would give him specific instructions on this very matter that was so urgently weighing upon his youthful mind.

The young Aviator was fervently reaching for the future. His full time mission was to be served from age nineteen to age twenty-one, the typical missionary age for young men in The Church of Jesus Christ of Latter-day Saints at that time. He was only thirteen years old, and he was already fretting and brooding over his future mission and future marriage. Emphasis on marriage. That's eternal. Missionary service is only two years.

God did answer the young Aviator's prayers concerning Dawn Lambert. One afternoon, as he lay on the couch to take a nap, he had an astonishingly vivid dream.

He dreamed that he had taken Dawn to Badger Mountain, a few miles east of East Wenatchee. His parents owned twenty-eight acres of meadow land in a small valley on Badger Mountain. His parents would take the family up there on outings from time to time.

In the dream, it was early afternoon on a serene day in late spring or early summer. The sun was shinning. A warm, gentle breeze swayed the tops of the tall, green grass and whispered softly through the pines on the hills surrounding the meadow. The sky was clear and blue. The Aviator had given Dawn a bouquet of flowers. After they had enjoyed their picnic lunch, Dawn and the Aviator lay side by side in the tall grass, holding hands and gazing up at the clear, blue sky. They drifted off to sleep in dreamy bliss.

Then, the dream took an abrupt and unexpected turn. The Aviator sat bolt upright in the grass. Dawn was missing. She was nowhere in sight. He called out to her, but she didn't answer. She was gone. Not like she had merely left the meadow, but more like she had completely vanished. The flowers the Aviator had so lovingly given her lay discarded and trampled on the ground a few feet away. The sky had turned ominously dark and cloudy, heavy, on the verge of rain. The warm, gentle breeze had become a fierce, cold wind. It chilled him to the bone. Sadness and emptiness permeated the air. The Aviator's heart sank.

Then, he awoke for real. The dream left him stunned and saddened and puzzled. But his love for Dawn did not fade.

Once, at a Church activity, he worked up the courage to give Dawn a single yellow flower he had picked outside the Church building. She acted sweet and thanked him. Minutes later, he saw her again in the hallway. She did not have the flower. As he rounded the corner of the hallway, a glint of yellow in the gray trash can caught his eye. He did a double take, and much to his chagrin, he saw the flower lying discarded in the trash, perched upon a pile of dirty paper plates and putrid, half eaten refreshments. His heart sank.

Still in love with Dawn, and still not getting the hints, the Aviator prayed all the more fervently for an answer from God as to whether or not this girl would be a good choice as a future wife. Why bother God about it when the answers are right in front of your face? Well, the young Aviator was stubborn like that.

God finally gave the Aviator an unmistakable answer. It was definitely not the answer the young Aviator wanted. But, it was the right answer, for more reasons than one.

Back in his day, before middle schools were organized, seventh, eighth and ninth graders went to junior high schools. Tenth, eleventh and twelfth graders went to senior high schools, just called high schools. The junior high school students were bussed to Wenatchee High School for swim lessons as part of the physical education program.

The Aviator attended Orchard Junior High School. He was in seventh grade at the time he got his answer about Dawn Lambert. It was late November or early December 1980.

One day, after changing in the locker room following swim class, the Aviator was sitting on a table near the drinking fountain, waiting for the rest of the class to gather for the school bus. He was in deep thought, pining for Dawn. Suddenly, he could not remember what she looked like. Worse, he could no longer feel the warmth and the love he had felt for her over the past several months.

All his feelings of fondness toward Dawn vanished in an instant, as if God had flipped a switch inside his heart and turned off a light inside his head. Try as he might, he could not rekindle his affections for Dawn. Every tender emotion he had ever felt for her was squelched forever, as if it had never existed. He could not even remember the feelings he had felt for her a few minutes prior. He felt empty and cold, just like in the dream.

This was the proverbial stupor of thought he had read about in the scriptures. The promise in the scriptures says that if you study a matter out in your mind, and then ask God if it is right, God will cause your heart to burn within you if it is right. But, if it is not right, God will give you a stupor of thought that will make you forget the thing that is not right.

The young Aviator got his answer straight from God. He knew it was an answer from God. No mistake about it. But, he could not help feeling heartbroken for many weeks.

Some time later, the Aviator received word through the Zitting family with whom Dawn had stayed in Wenatchee that Dawn had gone back East to her old boyfriend and her old life. That explained everything. The Aviator had no reason to feel heartbroken once he realized he hadn't lost anything after all. There had never been anything there to begin with. That's what God had been trying to show him all along.

Chapter Five

Frequently the brunt of scorn and ridicule, the Aviator was the type of kid almost everybody in school just had to tease. Among the most bothersome of hecklers was a cute, popular little girl named Kim Canterbury. Kim would poke fun at the Aviator on a daily basis during Mr. Leyden's seventh grade science class at Orchard Junior High School.

To get her off his back, the Aviator wrote her a pretend love letter. These are the words he wrote: Kim, why do you always make fun of me? You know I love you.

He passed the note to her on a folded piece of paper. By the end of the day, he could have had any girl he wanted. And Kim wanted to be his girl.

Kim apologized for her meanness and asked if they could go steady. He told Kim he could not date until he turned sixteen. Another one of those pesky youth standards his Church had taught him. But, as pesky and disheartening as it was to turn down such a golden opportunity, he remained firmly committed to his standards and kindly declined.

Kim could not understand at all, but she began to respect him and never again ridiculed him. Over the next few years, in high school, Kim suggested they get some other students together and make a movie starring the two of them. It would have been a romance adventure involving his flying skills and perhaps Kim as his romantic interest. The Aviator never made that happen. That was just one of many missed opportunities.

Girls would have been climbing all over him if only he had gone forward with Kim's movie idea. He could have written his own story in more ways than one. Hindsight is a real kick in the pants!

The young Aviator took a newspaper delivery route and any odd jobs he could find at age thirteen and started saving money for flying lessons. In spite of his shyness, he was fiercely determined. A few months after he turned fourteen, his adventures began.

Chapter Six

August 8, 1981 was a hot, summer day in the Wenatchee area. The Aviator asked his Dad to drive him to the airport for his first flight lesson.

His Dad drove him to Columbia Skyways, a fixed base operator (FBO) located on the northwest part of Pangborn Field in East Wenatchee. There, the young Aviator met his mentors.

Willard Skoglun owned the place and flew spray planes. Bill Saul was an amazing one-legged fellow who flew routine missions to Boeing Field, Seattle, for night cargo drops in a

Cessna-P210. The Aviator was later fortunate enough to ride along with Bill on several occasions. Sadly, some years later, Bill crashed near the summit of Mount Rainier. If memory serves correctly, Bill's body was never recovered.

Jim Watson became the Aviator's regular instructor. The Aviator knew Jim Watson from Civil Air Patrol. John Kell was the flight examiner and also happened to be the one who gave the Aviator his first flying lesson.

Following introductions all around, Dad said to the men, "I'm sure you'll be seeing a lot more of him."

That was intended to mean they would be seeing the Aviator quite frequently over the next several years. However, it turns out that the Aviator also saw John Kell at nearly every milestone in the Aviator's flying endeavors, from the Aviator's first flight lesson to his private pilot flight check nearly three years later, to his instrument rating flight check at Boeing Field nearly a decade later.

John Kell was a big fellow. He could barely fit into the small cockpit of the brown and white Cessna-152, tail number N48868. John walked the young Aviator through preflight procedures, pointing out the importance of draining water and sediment out of the fuel system with a handy little cup that had a metal pin sticking up from the middle to push open the fuel drain port under each wing and under the engine.

John demonstrated how to check the engine oil, the static port, and the Pitot tube. He showed the young Aviator what to look for while checking the cowl inlets, propeller blades, wing leading edge and wing surface, control surfaces, fuel tanks, and landing gear. They climbed into the cramped cockpit of the gutless Cessna-152, the Aviator in the pilot's seat and John in the copilot's seat. Learn by doing.

John instructed the Aviator on every detail of the checklist. The Aviator was soaking it up like a sponge. John pointed out that the brakes are activated by pushing your toes against the tops of the rudder pedals, and each brake can be operated independently to assist in ground handling.

After applying both brakes, starting the engine, and checking oil pressure, John told the Aviator to release the brakes and apply some throttle to begin taxiing. John demonstrated how to taxi the airplane using the rudder pedals, and then he let the young Aviator taxi the airplane out to the runway while John handled the radio, so the young Aviator could concentrate on operating the aircraft as he had been instructed.

Short of runway Two-Niner, they stopped, did engine run-up at 1700 rpm to check magnetos, carburetor heat, oil pressure, oil temperature, vacuum, and amperage. They verified all flight controls were free and deflected correctly throughout their full range of motion. They set the trim for takeoff, and then throttled back to idle.

After completing engine run-up, the fourteen-year-old Aviator felt a twinge of apprehension beneath the thrill of embarking on his long-awaited first flying lesson. He voiced this to John as they taxied onto the runway. "I've never done this before," he remarked to John.

"I know," replied John in a calm, matter-of-fact tone, as if to say don't sweat it, it's not that difficult.

Lined up on the centerline, John let the Aviator follow with hands on the controls. Full throttle, down the strip they went. This was exciting, especially for a geeky, unpopular misfit such as the young Aviator.

More than exciting, it was the beginning of a new chapter of his youth, his own coming of age, a transition from imagining to doing, from preparing to accomplishing, and from self doubt to confidence, at least where aviation was involved. Flying was at that moment officially and forever sealed into every fiber of his being. It became the driving force behind everything he did and everything he thought. No sacrifice was too great as long as it resulted in a few moments in the cockpit.

A bit of right rudder to keep the nose from drifting left due to engine torque and P-factor, slight back pressure on the elevators, keep ailerons more or less neutral, let airspeed build to sixty knots, then liftoff. Finally airborne!

They climbed at seventy knots on runway heading, and then made a gentle left turn, coordinating rudder and aileron, glancing at the ball on the turn-slip indicator, trying to keep it between the two lines for a properly coordinated turn. John demonstrated a few turns, and then let the Aviator try it. The young aviator felt so ecstatic, he had to muster at least as much concentration to contain his giddiness as he did to learn and practice the procedures John was teaching him. This was the first day of a long awaited quest.

Out over the Wenatchee Valley, they did a few more turns and then flew back to the airport to learn the approach pattern and landing procedures. John taught the young Aviator the appropriate radio calls and when to make them.

"Wenatchee Radio, Cessna Four-Eight-Eight-Six-Eight, inbound, three miles west of field, request winds and altimeter."

"Cessna Four-Eight-Eight-Six-Eight, Wenatchee Radio, winds three-three-zero at eight knots, visibility unlimited, altimeter two-niner-niner-four, runway Two-Niner is the active."

"Wenatchee Radio, Cessna Four-Eight-Eight-Six-Eight entering left downwind, runway Two-Niner."

John showed the Aviator how to configure for approach and landing and when to make the turns in the pattern. On the downwind leg, they reduced power to slow the airplane to about eighty knots and started configuring for landing.

Fuel valve verified open, mixture rich, primer locked, magneto switch set to both, carburetor heat off unless needed, master switch verified on, flaps ten degrees. They continued flying downwind until the approach end of the runway was behind the Aviator's left shoulder. At that point, they began a descending left turn to base leg.

"Wenatchee Radio, Cessna Four-Eight-Eight-Six-Eight, downwind to base, runway Two-Niner."

Flaps twenty degrees. Throttle 1500 RPM, airspeed sixty-five knots, trim adjusted for descent. With the end of the runway off the portside of the engine cowling, they started their turn to final and set flaps to the full thirty degrees of deflection. They closed the throttle for a power-off landing and trimmed the elevators to keep the attitude just right to maintain airspeed at sixty-five knots.

"Wenatchee Radio, Cessna Four-Eight-Eight-Six-Eight, base to final, Two-Niner."

John showed the Aviator how to stay on the glide slope by flying the airplane down to the runway while watching the visual approach slope indicator (VASI) lights on the ground at the sides of the approach end of the runway. Flying a normal glide path makes the far light appear red and the near light appear white. Both white, you're too high. Both red, you're too low.

Flying over the runway threshold, John demonstrated how to begin a gentle flare to let airspeed bleed off to sixty knots, then fifty. The object was to try to hold the wheels skimming just above the ground as long as possible, until just before the wing stalled.

John performed the first landing and let the Aviator follow with hands and feet on the controls. He showed the young Aviator how to stay quick on the rudder to keep the nose pointed down the runway. He showed him how to stay quick on the elevators without overcorrecting too much. It can be a bit of a challenge not to balloon and porpoise. It takes practice. If you can walk away, it was good enough.

They taxied off the runway and back to the tie-down area in front of Columbia Skyways. John taught the Aviator how to announce they had safely landed and taxied clear of the runway.

"Wenatchee Radio, Cessna Four-Eight-Eight-Six-Eight, down and clear of the active."

After shutting off the avionics and the tail beacon light, John showed the young Aviator how perform engine shutdown and how to secure the airplane. They ran the engine at 1200 RPM for about thirty seconds to prevent fowling of the spark plugs, and then pulled the mixture control to the lean position to kill the engine without leaving residual fuel in the cylinders. Starved of fuel, the engine sputtered to a stop, its death throbs making the instrument panel vibrate as if it were a living creature gasping for breath.

When the prop quit spinning, John told the Aviator to close the throttle and shut off the magnetos. Then, shut off the master switch. The Aviator loved the fading whine of the electric gyro wheel in the turn coordinator winding down after he shut off the master switch. There was something uniquely satisfying about it, a simple signature sound that rounded out the whole experience, imparting a sense of completion.

John told the Aviator to install the control lock to keep wind from whipping the control surfaces around. They set the parking break and exited the airplane.

With sweaty backs, the young Aviator and John tied down the airplane and walked across the hot flight line back to the Columbia Skyways office. Grinning from ear to ear, the young Aviator secretly began to glimpse just how awesome he really was. He might have seemed all nerd on the outside, but on the inside he was all Aviator.

To the young Aviator, such a simple event as a first flying lesson was a monumental achievement and an embarkation on a quest that would never die, no matter how old or feeble he would become. In his mind and heart, his quest would remain as bright and vibrant as the moment he strapped into that cockpit that hot August day. Ever refusing to give up hope amid future challenges, thoughts of aviation ever present in his mind, the Aviator would always say with youthful anticipation, "Life's not over yet."

DATE 1981	MAKE MODEL	REG. NUMBER	FROM / TO	PROCEDURES – MANEUVERS		AIRCRAFT SEL
8-8-81	Cessna 152	48868	WONALLEE LOCAL	Proficient, taxing, take off turns landing John C Hill OFI 1534874		5
8-31-81	C-152	48868	EAT EAT	Pattern, taxi, T.O & Ldg, turns, slow flite, stalls coordination CFII 165 7079 James W. Watson	00:21:51	9
9-5-81	C-152	48868	EAT Lol	T.O. & Ldg, Coordination, Slo Flite, Turns, Stalls Ted Ref Man 8FT 165 7079 James W. Watson		9
10-9-81	C-150	60754	EAT Lol	T.O. & Ldg, So Flite, stalls, sentinel acc CFII 165 7079 James W. Watson		1.0
10-31-81	C-152	N24887	EAT Lol	T.O. & Ldg, Slo Flite, Stalls, Sim Inst CFII 165 7079 James W. Watson		1.0
11-21-81	~~C-152~~	~~N34882~~	~~EAT Lol~~	~~Slo Flite, Stalls Ldgs Watson~~		1.0
12-19-81	C-152	N48868	EAT Lol			4
				PAGE TOTAL		5.7
				BROUGHT FORWARD		
				TOTAL		5.7

AIRCRAFT CATEGORY & CLASS		FLIGHT CONDITIONS					CROSS COUNTRY	PILOT TIME		TOTAL
SEL	MEL	DAY	NIGHT	INSTRUMENT				DUAL	P.I.C.	
				ACTUAL	HOOD	SIMULATOR				
5		6						5		5
9		9						9		9
9		9						9		9
1.0		1.0						1.0		1.0
1.0		1.0			3			1.0		1.0
1.0		1.0			2			1.0		1.0
4		4						4		4
5.7		5.7			.5			5.7		5.7
5.7		5.7			.5			5.7		5.7

John and the young Aviator entered the office to do the paperwork and start a pilot logbook for the Aviator. The other fellows in the office couldn't help but notice the sweat drenching the back of the young Aviator's shirt.

"Did you scare that boy, John?" asked Willard or Bill or Jim.

"He scared me," John laughed.

In the hours and days that followed that first flight lesson, the young Aviator replayed every sound, every sight, every motion, every procedure, every detail over and over again in his mind. He reflected on what he had learned. He ran thought simulations of what he needed to practice.

While reflecting on the thrill of beginning to realize his passion, the young Aviator began to notice how accurate his imagination had been while visualizing the flight characteristics of the airplane before actually flying it. Every sound, every vibration, the control pressures, the feel of the yoke, it was all exactly as he had imagined in his mind. Uncanny! This taught him something about the power of thought.

His passion was now much, much more than wishful thinking. He was alive and on fire. He worked harder and saved every penny, getting as many flights as he could, even if it was only once every two weeks or once a month. Soon, the young Aviator was spending extra time hanging out at the airport, washing and waxing airplanes in exchange for flight time.

Impassioned romantic that he was, the young Aviator took piloting airplanes to be far more than a mere mechanical exercise. It was a love affair. It was a passion that lifted his mind and heart to higher realms, making his spirit soar above the quagmire of mortal life.

Go on, dissect it and psychoanalyze it. Dismiss it as an overly romanticized, boyish fancy, or a phase or a fad, or label it as some bizarre type of obsession. Perceive it however you like.

The fact remains, the Aviator became a far better man than he ever would have become had he not developed such an intense passion and romance for aviation in his early years. His love for aviation had a character-shaping effect that was as profound as the spiritual growth he experienced during his two years as a full time missionary in Argentina.

Chapter Seven

The Aviator was a total albatross. He was awkward and clumsy in social situations. Almost every time he opened his mouth, he ended up embarrassing people around him as much as he embarrassed himself.

Around airplanes, however, he was in his element and felt perfectly at home. He came out of his shell and seemed a different person altogether. He was more at ease, more confident, sharp, and on top of his game. Through his experiences flying airplanes, he met people and talked with people he would never have approached had he not been a teenage pilot.

His ego got a much needed boost every now and then, allowing him to feel like a proud rooster for a few moments while out of his element. His first such proud rooster moment occurred the Sunday after his first flight lesson when he asked his scout master, Gary Moses, if Gary had taken radio calls from Cessna Four-Eight-Eight-Six-Eight on Saturday, August 8, 1981. Gary asked why. The Aviator proudly stated he was in that airplane taking his first flying lesson.

Gary Moses was a veteran Air Force fighter pilot who flew combat missions in Vietnam. Gary operated the Flight Service Station (FSS) at Pangborn Field throughout the Aviator's youth. The significance of that connection didn't click until the Aviator began interacting with Gary over the radio. The Aviator also became good friends with Gary's oldest son, Hunter, who was the same age as the Aviator.

When fellow boy scouts overheard the conversation Sunday at Church, they seemed surprised. Their surprise was a total ego swell for the Aviator. It seemed as though they were astonished that a mere timid nobody such as the Aviator would tackle something that required as much planning and discipline and competence as flying an airplane, particularly at such a young age.

Let's face it. The Aviator couldn't catch a football to save his life. He couldn't hit, catch, or throw a baseball or a softball. He couldn't keep track of a volleyball score or a basketball score. He couldn't get close to the girls without them thinking he was gross or weird or ugly.

Even grown-ups, like Wayne Lewis, thought he was overly sentimental for preserving his goldfish in alcohol after it died. That was in sixth grade. The Aviator dissected his goldfish in Mr. Babcock's science class at Columbia Elementary School. The dull scalpel did more mashing than slicing, so that was a bust. That was back when the Aviator had a crush on a girl named Kelly Standerford. The dissected goldfish didn't win any hearts.

The budding Aviator counted the money in his wallet in terms of flight hours rather than dollars. After all, why in the world would he ever consider spending so much as a dime on anything not directly related to getting off the ground?

And no, he never went to a prom. He nearly threw a duck fit when one of his friends mentioned spending 110 dollars on a prom date. What a raw deal. That was equivalent to three hours of cockpit time!

The Aviator's shirt pocket was usually packed with a calculator, flight navigation tools, and writing utensils, except at Church youth dances, when his pockets were topped off with snacks from the refreshment table where he spent most of the dance hanging out, trying to work up the courage to ask Roxanne, the foxy little girl of his dreams, to dance. He usually ended up feeling jealous and defeated and embarrassed for not taking the initiative when some other fellow stepped up and asked her to dance and she accepted without hesitation.

The unrequited yearning to have a girl with whom to share his adventures, even the adventures he created in his mind and heart, somehow inspired him to treat girls with chivalry and to esteem them with the highest regard. It also gave him incentive to work through life's difficulties and make things happen. He could hold a vision with unwavering clarity for as long as it took to make it a reality. After all, what good is a fantasy unless there is at least some possibility of making it come true?

The Aviator paid for his flight training with his own hard-earned wages. He often walked or rode his Dad's old, blue bicycle some ten miles from his home on South Chelan Street in Wenatchee to Pangborn Field in East Wenatchee. In other words, he would ride a bike for an hour or walk for almost three hours each way for a meager half hour of flight time.

Sometimes, he could catch a ride back to town with Jim Watson. But, even without rides to or from the airport, the long walk or bike ride would not have mattered to the Aviator. This was his life and his whole world.

He spent the trip out doing mental fight simulations in eager anticipation. He spent the trip back reflecting and reliving the thrill of the flight, and mentally retraining himself on maneuvers and procedures he identified as needing more practice and improvement.

A rough landing or a course correction or an uncoordinated maneuver was no cause for disappointment. It was all the more reason to look forward to the next flight to perfect the matter.

Eventually, that mentality paid dividends in both practical skill and accolades. Throughout his youthful quest to gain stick and rudder time in every different type of airplane he could afford to rent, various instructors complimented him on his piloting skills.

One winter, after Columbia Skyways had closed, the Aviator was getting checked out to rent airplanes from Executive Flight at Pangborn Field. After the Aviator greased in a couple of perfect landings, the instructor said, "I wish I could take credit for teaching you how to fly."

During an instrument training flight in a Piper PA-28-151 Warrior at Boeing Field in Seattle, the Aviator impressed his female instructor, Melissa Delvecchio. He got aggressive toward the localizer needle during an instrument landing system (ILS) approach in turbulent air. Each time the aircraft began drifting off the localizer, he immediately corrected the drift and flew the airplane back on course, keeping the needle centered right down to the runway.

"Great job!" remarked Melissa.

At one point, she changed her tune. The Aviator stayed on the glide slope until the runway threshold was well in view, and then reduced power and descended as if to land on the threshold. The low descent path alarmed Melissa.

"Oh, my...!" she exclaimed. The Aviator added power and arrested his descent in ground effect over the threshold and put the airplane down on the numbers.

His attention to detail scored him an awesome save while doing a preflight inspection of the Piper Warrior prior to an instrument training flight with Melissa. To this day, it remains a mystery to the Aviator whether the red shop rag he found inside the engine cowling had been accidentally left there by a maintenance worker, or deliberately placed by Melissa to test his thoroughness.

If it was a deliberate test, it was arguably more dangerous than any hot-dogging the Aviator had ever done. It would have been all too easy for an instructor to forget about that rag if the Aviator had not discovered it. A shop rag lying directly on the engine cylinder cooling fins would have caused a severe overheat, and likely a fire, shortly after takeoff.

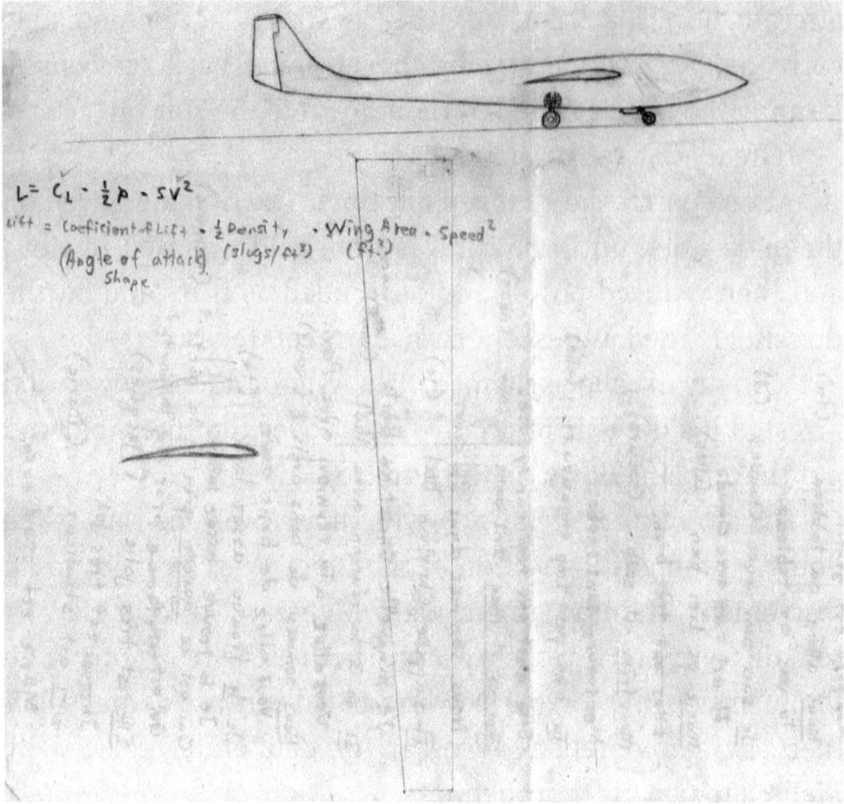

$$L = C_L \cdot \tfrac{1}{2}\rho \cdot S V^2$$

Lift = Coefficient of Lift · ½ Density · Wing Area · Speed²
(Angle of attack) (slugs/ft³) (ft²)
shape

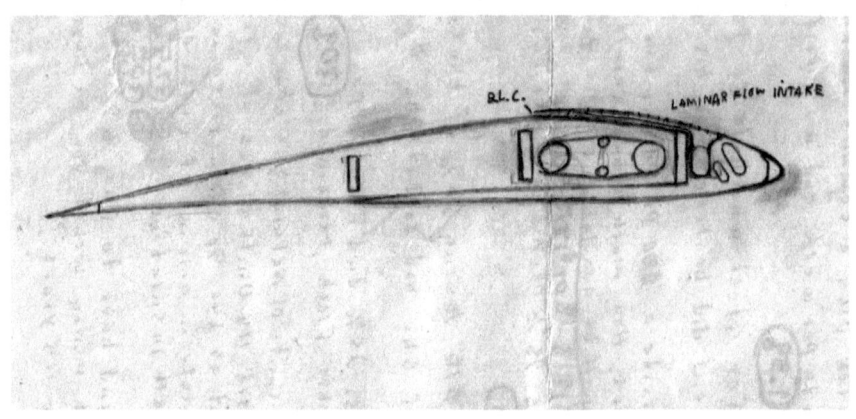

BLC   LAMINAR FLOW INTAKE

I. K. Lavanway — An Aviator At Heart

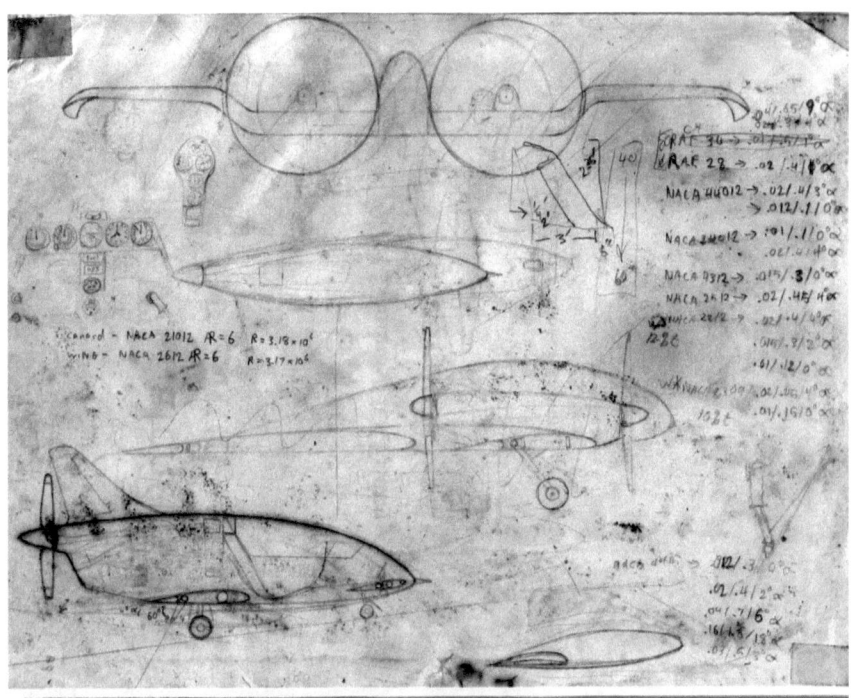

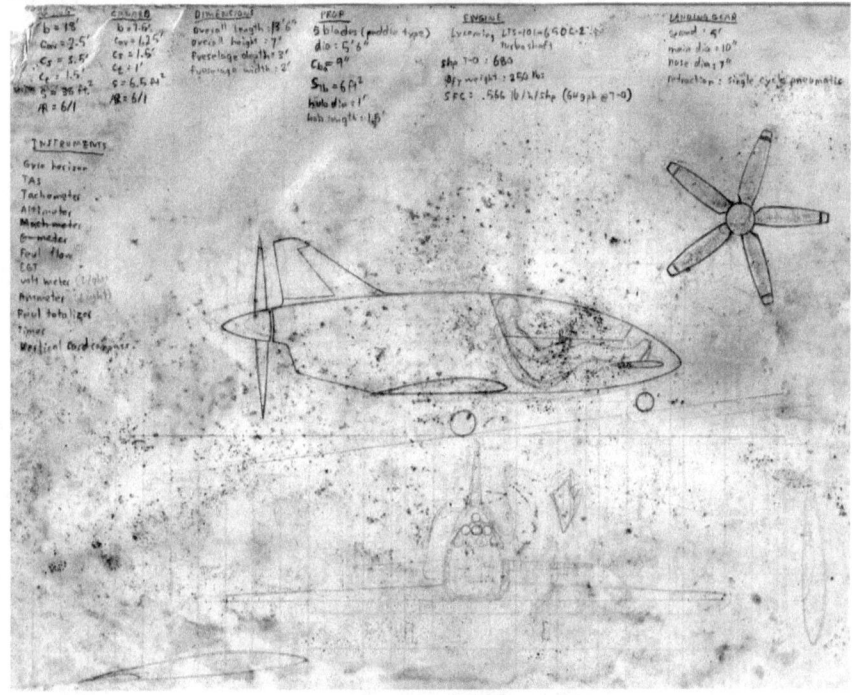

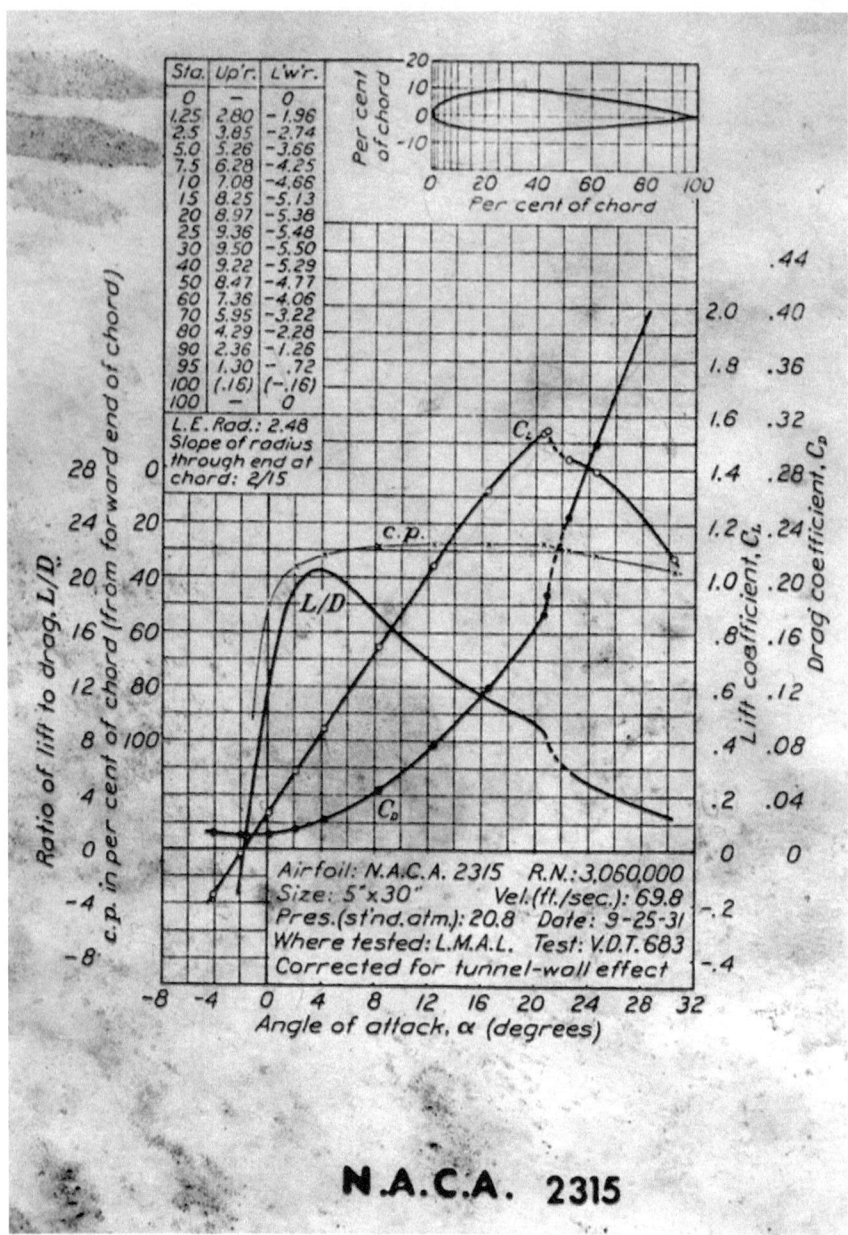

This sample was taken from a reference book in the early 1980s.
Title and author unknown.

CHAPTER EIGHT

Around age fourteen, the young Aviator taught himself to read lift curve slopes for different airfoils such as the Clark-Y and the similar USA-35B. He memorized the formulas for computing aerodynamic lift and drag in subsonic flight. He understood the effect of wing aspect ratio on induced drag and tip vortices. He understood why propellers were typically spun at speeds low enough to keep the blade tips from going supersonic. He understood that compressibility becomes an issue at higher speeds approaching the speed of sound.

On a couple of occasions, his thoughtful parents helped him get personal tours at the Boeing Company in the Seattle area, so he could ask questions to some of the Boeing aerospace engineers. Jay Farrell and another fellow named Stan were kind enough to talk with the young Aviator in their offices while his family was visiting Grandma in Seattle.

One winter, while the young Aviator sat at his Grandma's kitchen table pouring over a set of calculations for lift at different airspeeds and altitudes for a certain airfoil and wing area, his older cousin, Lee Whitney commented, "You look like an old man."

As a teenager, being called an old man was one of the greatest compliments the young Aviator had ever received. But, he was all nerd and quite juvenile when he walked into the Boeing engineers' offices and they kindly suggested he could take off his coat and relax.

"That's okay," he mumbled awkwardly.

He continued wearing his thick, bulky, hooded parka, even though the office rooms were comfortably warm and cozy. He produced his sheet of paper containing his lift calculations and asked if they were correct. The engineers looked them over for a while and said they looked right.

On a previous visit, the engineers had given him a Standard Atmosphere book to look up air densities at different altitudes. This helped tremendously. They explained a little about Reynolds Number. They answered his questions about induced drag. They explained how boat tail taper helps reduce aerodynamic drag on the aft fuselage of a jumbo jet.

On one visit, the engineers gave the young aviator pictures of the newly developed Boeing 767 and 757. They were promotional photos taken before the aircraft entered service.

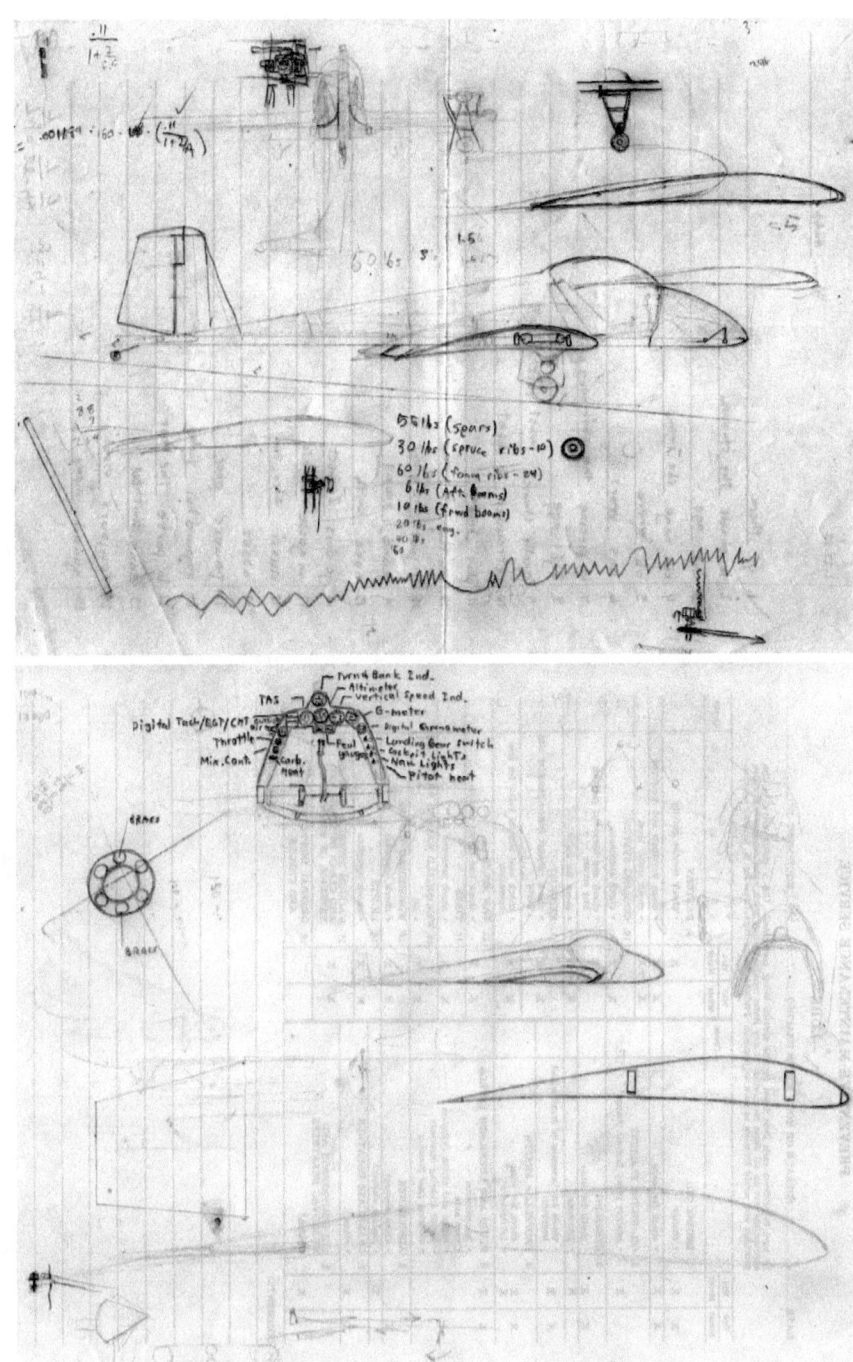

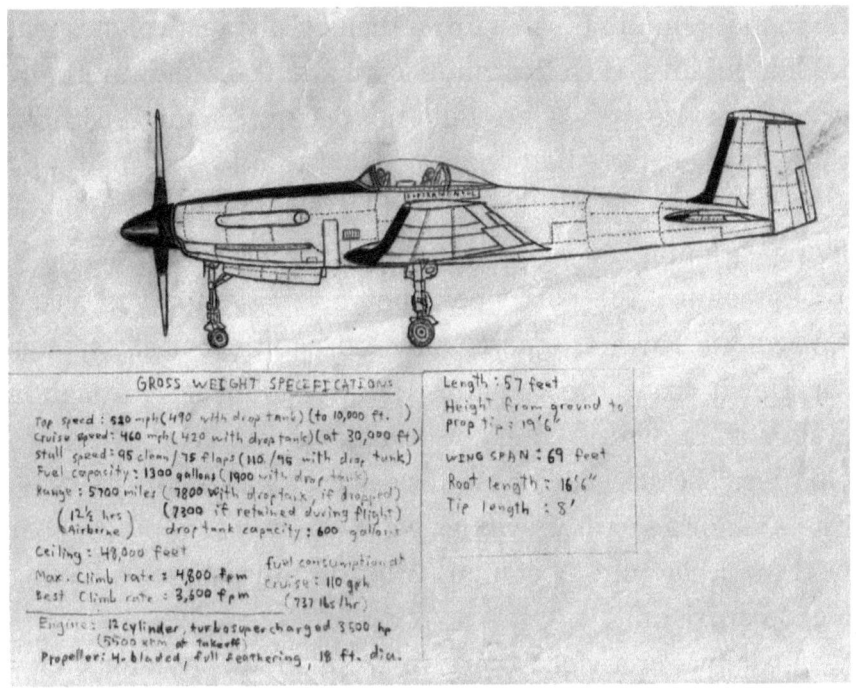

CHAPTER NINE

When the Aviator finally reached the ripe old age of fourteen, it was finally legal for him to attend Church youth dances. It didn't take him long to start noticing Roxanne Clay.

His fervent romance with flying was further fueled by his growing attraction to the foxiest little girl he had ever seen up to that point in his life. From then on, flying airplanes and falling in love with Roxanne could not remain mutually exclusive endeavors. One could not occupy his mind without the other, so they both occupied his mind continually. Of course, at some point he just had to take this wonderful girl flying with him.

Remember the part when the young Aviator had asked God about Dawn Lambert, and God had erased all feelings for Dawn from the Aviator's mind and heart through a stupor of thought? Well, the Aviator didn't stop talking to God just because he got an answer that sucked at the time. The Aviator's secret yearnings were counted as a prayer that God would let him meet a girl who was at least worth having a good crush on.

Roxanne was right there in front of the Aviator's face from the time they were both fourteen years old. The Aviator made his first real flight and met a new girl. What a year.

Over the next four years, Roxanne was never far away or out of reach. All the Aviator had to do was take the initiative, ask her out and make her his girl.

There she was, at dances, at Church conferences, at out-of-town high school debate tournaments, and at home with her parents in East Wenatchee. The Aviator's Mom occasionally bought Church literature from Roxanne's mom. Roxanne's mother had a Christian bookstore in the basement of her home.

Every time the Aviator's Mom needed Church books or supplies from Roxanne's mom, the Aviator would be all stoked and bursting at the seams with excitement for the opportunity to go to Roxanne's house. He was too shy to go over there on his own, although he would have been utterly mortified had anyone pointed that out to him. He would walk or ride a bike twice that distance to fly an airplane for half an hour. But, he wouldn't call Roxanne and ask if he could come over and spend a few hours with her. Wuss!

One incident was downright comical, at least in retrospect. It was a big deal at the time. This was still in eighth grade. The Aviator had been calculating and tabulating wing lift at different altitudes and airspeeds. He was excited about the fact that he could find books showing the lift curve slopes for various airfoil sections. He enjoyed looking up the lift coefficients corresponding to various angles of attack on a given airfoil's lift curve slope. He also made good use of that Standard Atmosphere book the engineers from Boeing had given him.

The Aviator was chafing at the bit to show off all his gnarly computations and sketches to Roxanne. So, when his Mom had to get supplies from her mom, the Aviator grabbed his files and got in the car, heart pounding with anticipation.

They got to Roxanne's house. While the mothers were downstairs doing business, the Aviator brooded for a few minutes and finally worked up an actual nerve or two. Mustering some pretense of confidence, he shyly asked, "Where's Roxanne?"

"Oh, she's upstairs, if you want to go talk to her." Hint. Hint.

Without another word, the Aviator raced up the stairs, rounded the banister into the living room, and was greeted by none other than Roxanne. Gasp!

"Um, Hi, Roxanne," said the Aviator, straining through his debilitating veil of shyness, heart pounding so hard he might have thought his sternum would rebound off his spine. "Um, wanna see some airfoil lift coefficients and standard atmosphere figures, and some airplane sketches?"

"Okay," said Roxanne, with a bit of a smile, trying not to giggle. Her smile and her attempt at a straight face accentuated her cute, foxy allure.

They walked over to the sofa and sat down next to each other. Roxanne's cute little legs could hardly reach the floor. They stuck out in front of her. She bounced happily and subtly.

Often, the Aviator was as dumb as a stump in social settings. But, he was also keenly observant of minutiae that others might miss or at best pass off as insignificant. Roxanne's adorable little antics drove him absolutely out of his mind.

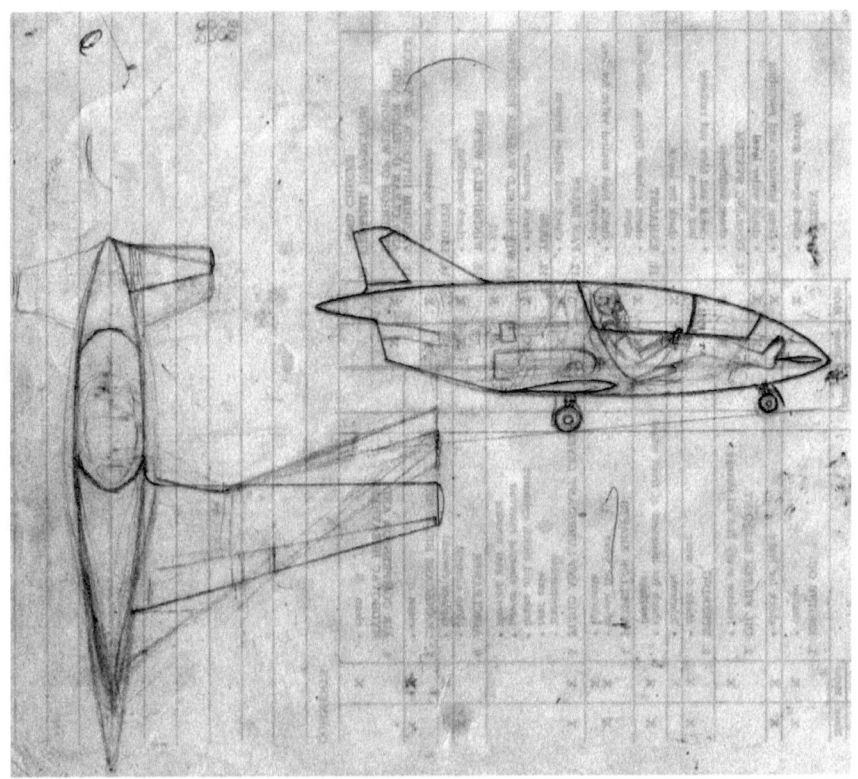

COMPUTING DRAG COEFFICIENTS OF DIFF. WING AR&.

$$C_D' = C_D + \frac{C_L^2}{\pi}\left(\frac{1}{A'} - \frac{1}{A}\right)$$

$$\alpha' = \alpha + \frac{C_L}{\pi}\left(\frac{1}{A'} - \frac{1}{A}\right)$$

α in radians

$L = C_L q S$

$q = \tfrac{1}{2}\rho r^2$

NOTE: These specifications are for the section USA 35-B only. They are given at an IR of 6 and are NOT corrected for tip vortices, root vortices, or any other complications. The wing planform is rectangular.

U.S.A. 35-B

CONVERSIONS: (approx.)
51.625 ft/sec = 35 mph
155.475 ft/sec = 106 mph
44.000 ft/sec = 30 mph
176 ft/sec = 120 mph
120.925 ft/sec = 82 mph
69.1 ft/sec = 47 mph
34.55 ft/sec = 24 mph
103.65 ft/sec = 70 mph
138.2 ft/sec = 94 mph
207.3 ft/sec = 140 mph

APRIL = 1982

C_L	α	$\rho \times 10^6$	ALTITUDE (ft)	V (in ft/sec)	°F	°C	Hg	LIFT (in lbs)	S (in ft²)
.4	0°	2377	S.L.	69.1	59.0	15.0	29.92	484	200
1.68	18°	2377	S.L.	69.1	59.0	15.0	29.92	1,907	200
1.68	18°	2377	S.L.	34.55	59.0	15.0	29.92	477	200
.4	0°	2308	1000	138.2	55.4	13.0	28.86	1,763	200
1.68	18°	2308	1000	34.55	55.4	13.0	28.86	462	200
1.68	18°	2308	1000	51.825	55.4	13.0	28.86	1,041	200
.4	0°	2241	2000	155.475	51.9	11.0	27.82	2,167	200
1.68	18°	2241	2000	44	51.9	11.0	27.82	729	200
.4	0°	2175	3000	155.475	48.3	9.1	26.82	2,103	200
1.68	18°	2175	3000	44	48.3	9.1	26.82	707	200
.4	0°	2111	4000	155.475	44.7	7.1	25.84	2,041	200
1.68	18°	2111	4000	44	44.7	7.1	25.84	686	200
.4	0°	2048	5000	155.475	41.2	5.1	24.90	1,980	200
1.68	18°	2048	5000	44	41.2	5.1	24.90	666	200
.4	0°	1755	10000	155.475	23.3	-4.8	20.58	1,697	200
1.0	8°	1755	10000	103.65	23.3	-4.8	20.58	1,885	200
.4	0°	1648	12000	176	16.2	-8.8	19.03	2,041	200
1.0	8°	1648	12000	120.925	16.2	-8.8	19.03	2,410	200
.4	0°	1496	15000	176	5.5	-14.7	16.89	1,863	200
1.0	8°	1496	15000	120.925	5.5	-14.7	16.89	2,187	200
.4	0°	1355	18000	176	-5.2	-20.7	14.94	1,678	200
.7	4°	1355	18000	138.2	-5.2	-20.7	14.94	1,810	200
.4	0°	1266	20000	176	-12.3	-24.6	13.75	1,568	200
.4	0°	1028	25000	176	-30.2	-34.5	11.10	1,273	200
.4	0°	889.3	30000	207.3	-48.0	-44.4	8.885	1,528	200
.4	0°	736.5	35000	207.3	-65.8	-54.3	7.041	1,265	200
.4	0°	585.1	40000	207.3	-69.7	-56.5	5.538	1,005	200
.4	0°	460.1	45000	207.3	-69.7	-56.5	4.355	790	200
.7	4°	460.1	45000	155.475	-69.7	-56.5	4.355	778	200
.7	4°	460.1	46000	176	-69.7	-56.5	4.355	998	200
.4	0°	362	50000	220	-69.7	-56.5		700	200

The Aviator opened his file folder and produced his work. He began explaining some of it. Roxanne politely and surprisingly seemed interested, or at least willing to listen. Whether she was truly interested in the technical details or just happy the Aviator was willing to share his passion with her was a bit of a mystery. But, the fact that she genuinely enjoyed the Aviator's company was a hint he never picked up on.

How was it that the Aviator could be so perceptive of practically indiscernible subtleties while at the same time he could be so obtuse and blind to the obvious? Was it part of his paradoxical mystique, or was he simply a turd?

All too soon, the mothers finished their transactions downstairs. The young Aviator's Mom called upstairs, "Are you ready to go, Son?"

"Um, I guess," groaned the Aviator, frustrated that he had only spent what seemed like a few minutes with Roxanne. He was just getting to the good part about how lift curve slopes drop abruptly after the critical angle of attack is exceeded and aerodynamic stall conditions occur, or some such subject.

The Aviator packed up his work, disappointment wafting over him, yet still too shy to say anything like: "No, Mom, I'm not ready to go. I haven't even kissed Roxanne yet. Don't you need some more books and stuff?"

The Aviator reluctantly went home with his Mom, pining for Roxanne all the way. Idiot!

CHAPTER TEN

After nearly two years of flying with instructor Jim Watson, the Aviator finally reached the legal age to be allowed to solo an airplane. Five days after turning sixteen, the Aviator made his first solo flight.

It was a clear, tranquil, spring day at Pangborn Field in East Wenatchee. Jim Watson flew with the Aviator for about half an hour for some final proficiency checks. Both felt confident in the Aviator's ability, so Jim told him to land the airplane on runway One-One. Jim exited the aircraft and told the young Aviator to take the airplane back up and do a few touch and go landings.

The Aviator taxied the Cessna-152 into takeoff position, set trim for takeoff, and smoothly advanced the throttle. In spite of the embarrassingly wimpy aircraft that is the Cessna-152, the experience of being in sole command of a real airplane was a thrill beyond words for this young Aviator.

The airspeed indicator reached sixty knots. With left fingers applying slight backpressure on the yoke, and right hand firewalling the throttle, the Aviator confidently flew the airplane off the ground. He was airborne, alone at last. Completely on his own, doing what he loved most.

The young Aviator reached pattern altitude, leveled off, and then turned downwind for his first solo landing. Getting an airplane off the ground and flying it are relatively easy tasks. Landing an airplane requires more concentration and forethought, and is potentially the most dangerous part of a flight. When done well, it is also among the biggest confidence builders.

DATE 1983	MAKE MODEL	REG. NUMBER	FROM / TO	PROCEDURES—MANEUVERS	AIRCRAFT SEL
4-8-83	C-152	48868	EAT / LCL	O.K. to Solo CFII-1657079 James W. Watson	.6
4-8-83	C-152	48868	EAT / LCL	Takeoffs & Landings Solo	.4
4-9-83	C-152	48868	EAT / LCL	O.K. to Solo 2nd time CFII-1657079 James W. Watson Solo	.3
4-9-83	C-152	48868	EAT / LCL		.7
4/14/83	C-152	48868	EAT / LCL	Solo Touch & Go Landings	.5
4/23/83	C-152	48868	EAT / LCL	Solo / coordination rolls, stalls	1:3
4/29/83	C-152	48868	EAT / LCL	Solo / stalls, slips, coordination rolls	1:2
			SPECIAL ENDORSEMENTS—BIENNIAL FLIGHT REVIEW—GROUND INSTRUCTION	PAGE TOTAL	5:0
				BROUGHT FORWARD	16:1
				TOTAL	21:1

AIRCRAFT CATEGORY & CLASS		FLIGHT CONDITIONS					CROSS COUNTRY	PILOT TIME		TOTAL
SEL	MEL	DAY	NIGHT	INSTRUMENT				DUAL	P.I.C.	
				ACTUAL	HOOD	SIMULATOR				
.6		.6						.6		.6
.4		.4							.4	.4
.3		.3						.3		.3
.7		.7							.7	.7
.5		.5							.5	.5
1:3		1:3							1:3	1:3
1:2		1:2							1:2	1:2
5:0		5:0						.9	4:1	5:0
16:1		16:1		2:1			16:1			16:1
21:1		21:1		2:1			17.0	4:1	21:1

Mid-field on the downwind leg, the Aviator did his pre-landing check. Fuel valve verified open, mixture rich, primer locked, magnetos both, carburetor heat on, master switch verified on, circuit breakers in, tail beacon on, landing light on, throttle to 1500 rpm, directional gyro set to match magnetic compass, flaps ten degrees, trim to compensate for flaps and reduced power, scan engine instruments, and scan for traffic in the pattern.

The Aviator developed his own habit of applying carburetor heat during descent, even when it wasn't needed. His overactive imagination visualized Venturi effect in the carburetor throat freezing moisture out of the air and icing up his carburetor, even on a good day.

Everything was smooth and familiar, but piloting the airplane suddenly became so much more thrilling, because it was all him, now. He was doing it. Things he had dreamed about and worked for during the past several years had finally come to fruition.

Every little procedure was a thrill in itself, like a note in a symphony, each detail synergistically adding to the creation of the whole experience, augmenting the overwhelming thrill of piloting a mass of metal through the air. Air, that invisible substance all around us that seems so thin and almost undetectable, but when moving through it fast enough, it bears up solid objects and feels as firm as rock.

The Aviator recalled how every sound, every sensation of movement, every control pressure in various flight conditions, all felt exactly as he had imagined it would when he was doing thought simulations back when he was thirteen years old and eagerly anticipating this very day. He remembered how he felt during his first flying lesson.

The Aviator looked out the portside window at the Pitot tube on the underside of the wing with the backdrop of terrain moving by. The sense of depth was breathtaking. He relished the sound of the slipstream and the rumble of the engine.

For some reason, that view in motion and the sounds and the feel of the controls in his hands all at once struck him to the core of his soul. It felt as if the airplane were an extension of his very being. He was free from the ground that had shackled him. This rivaled any other religious experience and surpassed most. It was as if he had suddenly seen himself. Words are inadequate for moments like this. It was just God and the Aviator, as Father and son.

"Wenatchee Radio, Cessna Four-Eight-Eight-Six-Eight, downwind, One-One," the Aviator announced, routinely.

The Flight Service Station radioed back wind speed, wind direction, and altimeter setting. The Aviator dialed in the current altimeter setting and mentally visualized the wind direction across the azimuth face of his directional gyro.

"Wenatchee Traffic, Cessna Four-Eight-Eight-Six-Eight turning right base, One-One." The Aviator banked right for a ninety-degree turn from downwind leg to base leg, putting him on a northerly heading, perpendicular to the runway. He set the flaps to twenty degrees and trimmed to compensate for the change in pitching moment, and to hold a descent rate of about five-hundred feet per minute at sixty-five knots.

"Wenatchee Traffic, Cessna Four-Eight-Eight-Six-Eight, right base to final, One-One, touch and go." He set the full thirty degrees of flaps and reduced power to idle, aligning the middle rivet on the cowling with the centerline of the runway. He executed a routine approach and a good landing. On rollout, he turned off the carburetor heat, dumped the flaps, re-trimmed for takeoff, and opened the throttle.

He lifted off for another couple of trips around the pattern before doing a full stop landing and taxiing triumphantly back to the flight line to report to his instructor. Jim signed the Aviator's logbook with the long-awaited proof that he was checked out for solo flight.

His first solo flight was by far the most thrilling experience in the young Aviator's life up to that time. He did not even have his driver license yet, and he could fly an airplane, solo. Kind of showed where his priorities were.

His peers were feverish over getting their driver licenses and getting cars. The Aviator had barely given any of that a second thought. Cars? What good are those, except for getting to the airport to rent airplanes?

He did get his driver license later that year. That proved invaluable in doing exactly what it was intended to do. It enabled him to get to airports to rent airplanes.

The Aviator completed his first solo flight in the same gutless Cessna-152 in which he had started flying lessons two years earlier. His solo flight was a milestone in his life. Now he could rent airplanes and fly by himself. He completed ground school, learned cross country flying, and became quite skilled at dead reckoning (deduced reckoning) navigation.

Chapter Eleven

The Aviator frequently rented an airplane and flew to Yakima to visit his Great Grandpa, Victor Elbert LaVanway. The diligent Aviator always filed a flight plan and took his sectional charts, even though he had the route, the radio frequencies, and the terrain memorized. He could make the flight day or night without a chart, but he never got in an airplane without one, unless he was just doing local flying around the Wenatchee area. A round trip flight from Wenatchee to Yakima and back took about an hour each way.

After landing in Yakima and tying down the airplane on the flight line at a Yakima FBO, the Aviator would walk from the Yakima airport to Great Grandpa's house. It was about a forty-minute walk at a brisk clip. He would usually visit for a few hours, and then walk back to the airport to fly the airplane back to Pangborn Field.

Great Grandpa was a mechanical genius who shared an interest in aeronautics. He once told the young Aviator about a memory from his youth.

"I used to watch how the snow swirled around the fence posts," Great Grandpa reminisced. Even as a kid, Great

Grandpa was interested in how wind currents reacted when they encountered solid objects.

Great Grandpa was skilled at hand carving small propellers. He gave a small, hand carved propeller to the young Aviator, June 15, 1970, when the young Aviator was only three years old. The Aviator still has that small propeller, engraved with his name and the date it was given to him by his Great Grandpa.

Some forty years later, the Aviator could still remember the smell of the wood smoke as Great Grandpa used a soldering iron to burn the writing into the little wooden propeller. He could still remember Great Grandpa rummaging through the tool shed in the back yard to find the soldering iron.

Great Grandpa invented a machine in the early 1900s that would automatically duplicate wooden propellers. He showed the machine to the Aviator, once. They had to drive out to meet the fellow who had purchased the machine from Great Grandpa some years prior. The machine still worked, and the Aviator got to see it operate. Great Grandpa also gave the Aviator a wooden propeller made on the machine. The Aviator still has that keepsake to this day.

On one flight to Yakima to visit Great Grandpa, the Aviator's dead reckoning skills surpassed his own expectations, resulting in another magnificent ego swell. The Aviator took off from Pangborn Field, landed in Yakima, spent the day with Great Grandpa, and then flew back to Pangborn Field. His wheels touched the runway at Pangborn Field at the exact minute of the estimated time of arrival (ETA) he had entered in his flight plan.

Later, Gary Moses, who was on duty at the Flight Service Station that day, told the Aviator: "I've never seen anybody nail a flight plan like that. You touched down exactly on your ETA." That made the Aviator's day. Made his whole week!

The Aviator had logged so many flights to Yakima that Willard Skoglun, the owner of Columbia Skyways, once asked the Aviator, "Have you got a girl in Yakima?"

"My Great Grandpa lives in Yakima," the Aviator explained, knowing that must have sounded like an excuse, even though it was the truth. He didn't know any girls in Yakima.

However, the Aviator did know a girl in Ellensburg. Cherene (Freenie) Clark. He had known her when they were both about two years old. He named her Freenie when he was two years old, because he could not pronounce Cherene. Her parents used to babysit him.

If memory serves correctly, only once in all his jaunts to Ellensburg and Yakima, did he ever pay a visit to Freenie. He flew over there to visit her at her high school one day. He talked to her for a few brief moments before she had to go to class. He never followed up with her, probably because he was head over heels for Roxanne. Mom asked if flying over to see Freenie was just a romantic notion. Probably. But what else would you expect from a hopeless romantic?

Sometimes, ordinary moments can produce some of the fondest memories. Some memories stand out for no particular reason. Maybe it's the way certain settings and small details combine to make an impression in the mind.

One ordinary day, after the Aviator had been checked out to fly four-seat Cessna-172 airplanes, Willard Skoglun was demonstrating how to use the newer avionics in one of the more upscale Cessna-172 airplanes. The Aviator thought it was cool how the Nav-Com radios allowed him to store standby frequencies and then, with the push of a little white, rectangular button, call up a standby frequency to active status. That reduced pilot workload when being handed off from en route communications with Center to a local tower, approach control, and then ground control.

After going over the newer avionics, Willard and the young Aviator were standing near the airplane. The airplane's reddish colored nose was jutting out of the hangar. The weather was clear and calm. The temperature was pleasant. The air was refreshing. The young Aviator was facing one side of the engine cowling, arms resting confidently atop the cowling. He was in his element, conversing with Willard about something related to the airplane.

Suddenly, everything felt unusually vivid and clear and familiar. It was not necessarily déjà vu. It simply felt like everything in that moment and in those surroundings fit together naturally. The young Aviator felt completely at home with all of this, this whole type of setting, like it was where he belonged, where he fit in, more or less, and definitely where he enjoyed being.

The only other places where the Aviator ever felt that way were later in life, in his own home and in the temples of The Church of Jesus Christ of Latter-day Saints. That's got to be one of those hints God keeps presenting.

Chapter Twelve

Jump back, way back to shortly after his first solo flight in 1983. The Aviator was out doing more solo flying. One particular day proved to be his first serious aviation adventure. If you have not already discerned it, you will soon discover that the word adventure in the Aviator's context often refers to experiences that are not merely exciting and memorable, but also laced with elements of danger, moderate degrees of hot-dogging, and mildly questionable legality.

It started out as a clear day. That changed quickly. The Aviator was tooling around the Wenatchee Valley, not paying attention to the deteriorating weather at Pangborn Field.

"Cessna Four-Eight-Eight-Six-Eight, Wenatchee Radio. Return to base immediately. Visibility half mile, rain and fog, winds light and variable. Use runway One-One."

"Roger, Eight-Six-Eight returning to base, ten northwest, inbound."

As the Aviator turned back toward Pangborn Field, he noticed the cloud ceiling and visibility had indeed dropped in the local vicinity of the airfield. Weather was fine just a few miles out, over the valley.

As he got closer to Pangborn Field, he had to continually descend to stay under the clouds. By the time he reached East Wenatchee, he was nearly down to treetop altitude. He decided to follow Grant Road east, from town to the approach end of runway One-One. The runway was almost perpendicular to Grant Road. The approach end of runway One-One was only a few dozen yards from the road.

The Aviator immediately put it in his mind that if could not acquire visual contact with the runway while flying up Grant Road, he would just land on the road, revel in the thrill of the experience, and take his licks for his poor situational awareness. He shot up Grant Road at full throttle, skimming along at about one-hundred feet above ground level, doing around 110 knots.

He planned his low level approach impromptu. He shot passed the approach end of One-One at full power, cranked the airplane into a nearly ninety-degree degree left bank and hauled on the yoke, pulling about three Gs.

In a sixty-degree bank, it takes two Gs to maintain altitude. At nearly ninety degrees of bank, three Gs is not enough to hold altitude, but a slight descent was in order at this point, anyway. As the Aviator flew this highly unconventional, dangerous, low-level approach pattern of his own making, he reduced power in the turn, bled off airspeed by maintaining a steep bank and a high load factor, and eased in the fist notch of flaps.

Coming around so the approach end of the runway was in sight on his left, he eased in another notch of flaps, reduced his bank somewhat, and added some power to hold altitude in the turn. As he completed his 270-degree turn and lined up the approach end of the runway with one of the rivets on his engine cowling, the Aviator reduced power and applied full flaps. The rain was torrential. The runway was barely visible. These were no longer VFR conditions. If anyone squawked, the Aviator could just say he was IFR: I Followed Road.

Straining his eyes and moving his head around to keep a visual on the runway through the pouring rain, he greased in a sweet landing and taxied to Columbia Skyways flight line. No sooner had he shut down his engine, than he felt someone grab the tail of the aircraft and begin pulling it backward into the tie-down spot. Jim Watson and John Kell tied the airplane down, getting drenched to the bone in the downpour. The Aviator got out and was greeted by a scolding.

"I hope you learned something out there, young man!" shouted Jim.

"Yes, Sir," replied the Aviator. The Aviator was happy to be down safely, having learned that weather can change drastically, without warning. Just because weather is clear in one place does not mean it is still good a few miles away.

In spite of the scolding, secretly, the Aviator was uber pumped. That was the coolest bit of flying he had done up to that time in his life.

CHAPTER THIRTEEN

After completing ground school, the Aviator passed his private pilot written exam. While it was legal to solo at age sixteen, the minimum age for receiving a private pilot license was seventeen. That seemed like an eternity to the young Aviator. He was more than ready.

The year 1984 had to be one of the best years, if not the best year of this Aviator's youth. On the day he turned seventeen, the Aviator passed his private pilot flight check and received his private pilot license.

DATE 1984	MAKE MODEL	REG. NUMBER	FROM / TO	PROCEDURES — MANEUVERS
3-3-84	C-152	48868	EAT / LCl	Takeoffs & Landings, Stalls, coordination
3-6-84	C-152	48868	EAT / LCl	Sim. Inst. T.O.&Lag (Nite) (S) CFI-1657079 James W. Watson
3-21-84	C-152	48868	EAT / LCl	Sim Long Approach & App. T.O.&L&g (S) CFI-1657079 James W. Watson
3-26-84	C-152	48868	EAT / LCl	Sim. Sto Flite, T.O.&Ldgs Nite (S) CFI-1657079 James W. Watson
3-31-84	C-152	48868	EAT / LCl	Sim Rcov Sto Flite, Stalls, Turns, T.O.&Ldgs CFI-1657079 James W. Watson
4-2-84	C-152	48868	EAT / LCl	Turns, Stalls, Takeoffs & Landings
4-3-84	C-152	48868	EAT / Roney	Private Pilot — Ride SATISFACTORY Ed O Keel S-66 SPE

SPECIAL ENDORSEMENTS — BIENNIAL FLIGHT REVIEW = GROUND INSTRUCTION

	PAGE TOTAL	5.9
	BROUGHT FORWARD	62.8
	TOTAL	68.7

AIRCRAFT CATEGORY & CLASS			FLIGHT CONDITIONS					CROSS COUNTRY	PILOT TIME		TOTAL
SEL	MEL		DAY	NIGHT	INSTRUMENT				DUAL	P.I.C.	
					ACTUAL	HOOD	SIMULATOR				
.5	:	:	.5	:	:	:	:	:	:	.5	.5
1.0	:	:	:	1.0	.7	:	:	:	1.0	:	1.0
1.0	:	:	:	1.0	.8	:	:	:	1.0	:	1.0
1.0	:	:	:	1.0	:	:	:	:	1.0	:	1.0
1.0	:	:	1.0	:	.6	:	:	:	1.0	:	1.0
.4	:	:	.4	:	:	:	:	:	:	.4	.4
1.0	:	:	1.0	:	.2	:	:	:	:	1.0	1.0
5.9	:	:	2.9	3.0	2.3	:	:	:	4.0	1.9	5.9
62.8	:	:	62.8		:	2.4	:	33.8	22.8	40.0	62.8
68.7	:	:	65.7	3.0	:	4.7	:	33.8	26.8	41.9	68.7

You know what that meant; finally, he could take passengers. In other words, he could give Roxanne an airplane ride. But, the shy Aviator took his sweet time working up the courage to ask her. In fact, the very opportunity that had been featured in so many of his daydreams was miraculously presented to him one day, when he was least expecting it. We'll get to that.

On one occasion, the Aviator got some free flight time when Willard Skoglun asked him to fly a Cessna-172 out to Yakima to pick up a fellow who was one of Willard's customers and fly him back to Pangborn Field. The Aviator didn't have a commercial rating, so Willard told the Aviator, "Just tell him you're doing me a personal favor, and he doesn't need to pay the commercial rate."

The shy, seventeen-year-old Aviator felt it was an honor to be entrusted with the responsibility of flying to pick up a passenger for Willard. Adding to the significance of the experience was the fact that the Aviator had never met the passenger previously, and the passenger trusted the kid pilot based on Willard's recommendation.

On another occasion, the Aviator flew his Dad out to visit Dad's old Army buddy, Andy Slinkard, who had a ranch with a private dirt airstrip located about three miles northwest of Mesa, Washington. The Aviator landed the airplane on the dirt strip near Andy's house. The airstrip was basically a widened out segment of a dirt road than ran diagonally across a field.

During takeoff from the dirt strip, the Aviator relished the simple thrill of blasting through the irrigation sprinkler spray arching across the airstrip. The airstrip was narrow.

Tall grass lined the sides. The Aviator had to jab right rudder a bit to keep the left wheel from sinking into the soft dirt along the left side of the strip. Grass whipped the wheel fairing.

After returning the aircraft to Pangborn Field, Jim Watson approached the Aviator and asked, "Did you land this thing on a grass strip somewhere?"

"Uh.., not exactly. Why?"

"We found grass stuck in one of the wheel fairings."

"Oh, I got a bit too close to the edge of the strip out there. There was a lot of grass along the sides, and it was a narrow strip. Must have caught some on takeoff."

"Well, don't go landing on grass strips."

"No problem."

Technically, it wasn't a grass strip. It was a dirt strip. And it wasn't a problem. It was a skill-honing experience that would the serve young Aviator well in times to come. Plus, it was a fond memory, and a confidence builder.

Many a time, adults urged the shy Aviator to take initiative in life. The things he did with airplanes were probably not what they had in mind. No doubt, God stepped in more than once to keep the daring young Aviator out of serious trouble.

Chapter Fourteen

Over the months since the young Aviator earned his private pilot license, he occasionally borrowed his parents' car, an orange, 1970s era Plymouth Scamp. He drove from Waterville to Ellensburg, about a two-hour drive.

He knew a lady in Ellensburg from Civil Air Patrol who owned an old, white Cessna-172, tail number N1696Y. She was kind enough to let the Aviator rent it for twenty dollars per hour of engine time, wet rate. Wet rate means fuel and oil are included in the rental cost. That was dirt cheap, even back then.

He would occasionally go to Ellensburg, rent that airplane, and fly it back to Waterville and East Wenatchee for the weekend. Since he only had to pay for engine time, he could keep the airplane for two or three days at a stretch. From Waterville and East Wenatchee, he would fly that old beater plane all over the state, racking up cross country flight time and many adventures.

One of his fondest memories was of a time in Waterville, in the pre-dawn hours. The Waterville airport was only a few blocks from the Aviator's house. He had rented the old

Cessna-172 from Ellensburg and flown it home. He kept it for about three days.

In the wee hours one morning, he decided to go up for a night flight. It was about 0300 hours. He grabbed his headset and walked out into the peaceful night air. Everything was still and tranquil.

In spite of the hour, he felt alive, invigorated, and clear headed. It was one of those moments that can't be adequately described, but it created a most pleasant memory. The sound of gravel under his feet as he walked out to the airstrip. The cool, refreshing, night air. The clear, black sky. The hush over the town and the fields. All underpinned by a sense of total and complete freedom, and the thrill of having an airplane at his sole disposal. He breathed it all in as if it were a lifetime, a good life, a fulfilling life, encompassed in the span of a few minutes.

Flying in the still, night air was so peaceful it was almost surreal. There was no turbulence. There was something awe-inspiring about the glint of the aircraft's floodlight on the back of the spinning propeller. It illuminated a transparent disk ahead of the cockpit, particularly visible when looking out the pilot side window, forward and slightly downward. The illuminated arc traced out by the prop tip was starkly contrasted against the black of night.

The steady drone of the engine sung the song of this young Aviator's heart. The slipstream lulled his mind. The controls felt smooth, alive, solid, yet compliant to his hands and feet. A sense of being motionless, suspended in space, belied the fact that he was hurling through the air in a metal contraption at over a hundred knots.

DATE 19 84	MAKE MODEL	REG. NUMBER	FROM ↑ ↓ TO	PROCEDURES – MANEUVERS	AIRCRAFT SEL
7/7/84	C-172	N1696Y	ELN Local	A/C check Ride in SAR plane OK to use Bruce A. Potter CFI 271686 797 EXP-2-28-86	:8
7/7/84	C-152	48868	EAT-ELN-EAT	cross country	1:0
7/8/84	C-172	4844J	EAT-PUW-EAT	cross country	3:2
7/18/84	C-172	1696Y	ELN-PUW-OKN-ELN	cross country	4:4
7/26/84	C-152	48868	BAT-KENNEWICK-EAT	cross country	2:0
8/4/84	Beech 7K	2583E	VANC Local	Bis Hards Mint CFI 201337	1:7
8/4/84	C-172	1696Y	ELN-CHEHALIS	cross country	1:5
				PAGE TOTAL	14:6
				BROUGHT FORWARD	92:2
				TOTAL	106:8

AIRCRAFT CATEGORY & CLASS		FLIGHT CONDITIONS					CROSS COUNTRY	PILOT TIME		TOTAL
SEL	MEL	DAY	NIGHT	INSTRUMENT				DUAL	P.I.C.	
				ACTUAL	HOOD	SIMULATOR				
:8	:	:8	:	:	:	:	:	:8	:	:8
1:0	:	1:0	:	:	:	:	1:0	:	1:0	1:0
3:2	:	3:2	:	:	:	:	3:2	:	3:2	3:2
4:4	:	4:4	:	:	:	:	4:4	:	4:4	4:4
2:0	:	2:0	:	:	:	:	2:0	:	2:0	2:0
1:7	:	1:7	:	:	:	:		1:7	:	1:7
1:5	:	1:5	:	:	:	:	1:5	:	1:5	1:5
14:6	:	14:6	:	:	:	:	12:1	2:5	12:1	14:6
92:2	:	87:3	4:9	:	4:7	:	49:5	28:8	63:6	92:2
106:8	:	101:9	4:9	:	4:7	:	61:6	31:1	75:7	106:8

DATE 1984	MAKE MODEL	REG. NUMBER	FROM → ↓ TO	PROCEDURES – MANEUVERS		AIRCRAFT SEL
6-1-84	C-152	48868	EAT YKM	cross-country		.7
6-2-84	C-152	48868	YKM EAT	cross-country		.7
6-22-84	C-172	48945	EAT – YKM EAT	cross-country		1:4
6-27-84	C-152	48868	EAT Lcl	takeoffs & Landings		.6
7-4-84	AROUCA 7-AC	25852	VANC LOCAL	Stpturns stalls-durnoles-logs Gary W. B. fl 5520285458CE1884	3	.7
7-4-84	T-CRAFT BC-12D	96202	VANC LOCAL	Ldings, x-wind Gary W. B. fl 5520285458CE1884	6	.7
7-4-84	C-152	48869	EAT – PDX EAT	cross-country, dutch rolls		4:0
			SPECIAL ENDORSEMENTS – BIENNIAL FLIGHT REVIEW – GROUND INSTRUCTION		PAGE TOTAL	8:8
					BROUGHT FORWARD	83:4
					TOTAL	92:2

AIRCRAFT CATEGORY & CLASS		FLIGHT CONDITIONS					CROSS COUNTRY	PILOT TIME		TOTAL
SEL	MEL	DAY	NIGHT	INSTRUMENT				DUAL	P.I.C.	
				ACTUAL	HOOD	SIMULATOR				
.7		.7					.7		.7	.7
.7		.7					.7		.7	.7
1:4		1:4					1:4		1:4	1:4
.6		.6							.6	.6
.7		.7						.7		.7
.7		.7						.7		.7
4:0		4:0					4:0		4:0	4:0
8:8		8:8					6:8	1.4	7.4	8:8
83:4		78:5	4.9		4:7		42.7	27.2	56:2	83:4
92:2		87:3	4.9		4:7		49.5	28.6	63.6	92:2

Chapter Fifteen

Another favorite adventure included flying over the Cascade Mountains to a small airfield located at the corner of Southeast Mill Plain Road and 136th Avenue, Vancouver, Washington. This little airfield was called Evergreen Field.

The young Aviator had heard about a rather unique FBO there, nestled like a sanctuary amid the suburban sprawl. At Evergreen Field, he eagerly expanded his repertoire, flying 1940s era taildraggers including an Aeronca 7AC Champ, tail number 2583E, and a Taylorcraft BC-12D, tail number 96202. The owner of the airfield was the rather famous Wally Olson.

The young Aviator's first flight to Evergreen Field was in a Cessna-152 he had rented from Columbia Skyways. On the Fourth of July, 1984, he made an early morning departure from Pangborn Field. He wanted to spend the day flying taildraggers and still have daylight to enjoy the mountain scenery while flying home.

As you may know, western Washington is often foggy during the morning hours. The Aviator discovered en route that it was still too foggy to land VFR at Evergreen Field. As he scoured the terrain below, he found an alternate landing site at a grass airstrip used by the forest service.

He landed safely and shut down his engine. His sense of accomplishment at having executed an impromptu landing at a small, unfamiliar airstrip in the hills was interrupted by one of his pesky, chronic nosebleeds. It was a gusher. His face might have looked like something out of a slasher flick.

As he got out of the airplane, he was greeted by a few surprised forest service crewmen. He probably woke them up when he landed. They were surprised to see a kid on an early morning cross country flight drop in barely an hour after sunrise to wait out some fog. They seemed impressed that he was able to land his airplane safely on their small, grass airstrip. One of them even asked, "How did you find this place?"

The Aviator explained that he had noticed it from the air. It seemed like a good place to set down until the fog cleared at his intended destination.

His pride got slapped around like a red-headed step child when they noticed him nursing his hemorrhaging nose. One of the forest service crewmen suggested the bloody nose was due to nervousness. No way!

First, the Aviator wasn't really that nervous. Pumped up with an adrenaline rush from performing an unplanned, short-field landing on a secluded, grass runway? Yes. Nervous? No.

Second, he had a history of chronic nosebleeds. No apparent reason. It could happen to him any time, day or night. It was more embarrassing than alarming. But, trying to talk this one down was only going to dig the pit of embarrassment deeper. He just kept pinching his nose. Eventually, it stopped bleeding.

The crewmen offered him some coffee while he waited. He explained that he was raised in The Church of Jesus Christ of Latter-day Saints and was taught to avoid coffee. That standard is part of the Word of Wisdom. He asked if they had any hot chocolate, instead. They did, and it tasted great. The always-hungry teen Aviator restrained his urge to Bogart their entire stash.

He asked to use their phone to update his flight plan for a later arrival at Evergreen Field. He also got weather updates.

The forest service crew showed the young Aviator their helicopter. Unfortunately, the Aviator didn't succeed in talking them into giving him any flight instruction in it. Massive bummer.

After a couple of hours and a few more weather checks, he was happily airborne again. Short-field and soft-field takeoff procedures. Actual application. The way it was meant to be.

Flaps twenty degrees, full throttle, yoke all the way back, get the nosewheel off the grass, heavy right rudder, fifty-five knots, liftoff. Ease the flaps up while building airspeed. Point the nose in the specific direction of Evergreen Field and get some more awesome flying done. Where were the girls when all this studliness was happening?

The Aviator made it safely to Evergreen Field and had a swell day. There are probably not many airfields like that left in America. Places where a kid with a sense of nostalgia and a passionate aversion to the ground can afford to fly airplanes from an era that matched his anachronistic taste in music and his old-fashioned air of chivalry. Places where a kid can get schooled by legendary pilots like Wally Olson.

DATE 19 84	MAKE MODEL	REG. NUMBER	FROM / TO	PROCEDURES – MANEUVERS	NO. of Landings takeoffs	AIRCRAFT SEL
8/4/84	C-172	1696Y	CHEHALIS → VANC.	cross-country		.8
8-5-84	ARONCA 7-AC	2583E	VANC → LOCAL	LANDINGS, X-WIND, CHECKOUT OK Sayer & Hansen Cessna E-30-86 full-stop	full stop 10 Landings P.I.C.	3.4
8-5-84	ARONCA 7-AC champ	2583E	VANC → Lcl	cross-wind landings & takeoffs (2)		.2
8-8-84	T-craft	96202	VANS → Lcl	checkout / Olsen C/8/4/51		.4
8-6-84	Taylorcraft	96202	VANS → Lcl	slow flite, stalls, takeoffs & landings	(7)	.9
8-6-84	C-172	1696Y	VANC → KENNEWICK	cross-country		1.5
8-6-84	C-172	1696Y	KENNEWICK → ELN	cross-country		.9
			SPECIAL ENDORSEMENTS – BIENNIAL FLIGHT REVIEW – GROUND INSTRUCTION		PAGE TOTAL	8.1
					BROUGHT FORWARD	106.8
					TOTAL	114.9

No. of Landings	AIRCRAFT CATEGORY & CLASS		FLIGHT CONDITIONS						PILOT TIME		TOTAL
	SEL	MEL	DAY	NIGHT	INSTRUMENT			CROSS COUNTRY	DUAL	P.I.C.	
					ACTUAL	HOOD	SIMULATOR				
	.8	:	.8	:	:	:	:	.8	:	.8	.8
10 Landings P.I.C.	3.4	:	3.4	:	:	:	:		2.0	1.4	3.4
	.2	:	.2	:	:	:	:		:	.2	.2
	.4	:	.4	:	:	:	:		4	:	.4
(7)	.9	:	.9	:	:	:	:		:	.9	.9
	1.5	:	1.5	:	:	:	:	1.5	:	1.5	1.5
	.9	:	.9	:	:	:	:	.9	:	.9	.9
	8.1	:	8.1	:	:	:	:	3.2	2.4	5.7	8.1
	106.8	:	101.9	4.9	:	4.7	:	61.6	31.1	75.7	106.8
	114.9	:	110.0	4.9	:	4.7	:	64.8	33.5	81.4	114.9

DATE 19 84	MAKE MODEL	REG. NUMBER	FROM ↑ ↓ TO	PROCEDURES — MANEUVERS	AIRCRAFT SEL
9-1-84	C-172	1696Y	ELN — WNTRAVILLE	x-country, steep turns	1.1
9-1-84	C-172	1696Y	WNTRAVILLE — Grand Cou	x-country	2.5
9-1-84	C-172	1696Y	BAT — VANC.	x-country	2.4
9-2	Taylorcraft	96WV	VEO tcf	checkout Allen Cessna	.2
9-2-84	Taylorcraft	96202	VANC. Lcl	Takeoffs & Landings (rough field)	.3
9-2	A28 140	723J	VAN tct	stalls, glider tows check out Allen Cessna 139748	.9
9-2	PA 28-140	723J	VANC lcl	Stalls, takeoffs & Landings, steep turns (rough field)	.8
				PAGE TOTAL	8:2
				BROUGHT FORWARD	114:9
				TOTAL	123:1

AIRCRAFT CATEGORY & CLASS		FLIGHT CONDITIONS					PILOT TIME		TOTAL
SEL	MEL	DAY	NIGHT	INSTRUMENT			CROSS COUNTRY	DUAL	P.I.C.	
				ACTUAL	HOOD	SIMULATOR				
1.1	:	:	1.1	:	:	:	:	1.1	:	1.1	1.1
2.5	:	:	2.5	:	:	:	:	2.5	:	2.5	2.5
2.4	:	:	2.4	:	:	:	:	2.4	:	2.4	2.4
.2	:	:	.2	:	:	:	:	:	2	:	.2
.3	:	:	.3	:	:	:	:	:	:	.3	.3
.9	:	:	.9	:	:	:	:	:	.9	:	.9
.8	:	:	.8	:	:	:	:	:	:	.8	.8
8:2	:	:	8:2	:	:	:	:	6:0	1:1	7:1	8:2
114:9	:	:	110:0	4:9	:	4:7	:	64:8	33:5	81:4	114:9
123:1	:	:	118:2	4:9	:	4:7	:	70:8	34:6	88:5	123:1

During August and September 1984, Wally Olson flew with the young Aviator to check him out for solo flight in the old Taylorcraft and in a Piper PA-28-140 Cherokee. While flying the Taylorcraft, the Aviator enjoyed doing full-stall landings. He learned to hold the wheels just above the runway and bleed off speed, gradually easing back on the yoke to increase the wing's angle of attack just enough to stall it and plant the tailwheel on the ground a spilt second before the main gear touched down. That was awesome!

While flying with Wally to get checked out in the Piper Cherokee, the young Aviator greased in a perfect landing. It was so smooth, the only way to know the wheels had actually contacted the runway was by hearing and feeling the vibrations as they rolled over the rough, uneven, narrow, paved airstrip that ran parallel the grass airstrip the taildraggers normally used. As the Aviator dumped the flaps, opened the throttle, and re-trimmed the airplane for takeoff, Wally told him, "There's no doubt about your ability to fly an airplane. Give me one more like that."

To the nerdy, seventeen-year-old Aviator, such a compliment coming from Wally Olson meant a lot. That made his day. Made his whole week!

Wally Olson was a well known and well seasoned pilot, one of the great old pilots who had been around since before World War II. Wally had owned and operated Evergreen Field since 1945. The young Aviator didn't learn about that bit of history until almost three decades after he met Wally.

There are probably many news and history articles out there about Wally Olson and Evergreen Field. During the summer of 1984, the adolescent Aviator was unaware of the historical significance of the people and places with which he was interacting. After all, his head was in the clouds, both literally and figuratively.

When it came to flying the Aeronca Champ, the juvenile Aviator was in absolute heaven. This was old school stick and rudder. He learned to hand prop the engine on the Champ and the Taylorcraft. These old planes had no starters in them. No electrical systems whatsoever.

In the Aeronca Champ, the seats were tandem, rather than side by side. The brakes were located on the outboard sides of the heels of the rudder pedals, and they barely worked. The flight control stick was an actual stick, not a yoke.

The instrument panel was sparsely populated with the bare minimum gauges: airspeed, altimeter, turn-slip indicator, magnetic compass, tachometer, oil pressure, and oil temperature. There were no onboard radios or lights. This was pure seat-of-the-pants flying.

Fuel quantity was indicated by a metal wire attached to a float inside the thirteen-gallon fuselage tank that sat between the firewall and the instrument panel. The metal wire protruded through a hole in the top of the fuel filler cap right smack in front of the cockpit. The wire would bounce up and down wildly, so you had to estimate your fuel based on the average height of the bouncing wire. Or start out with a full tank, and then time your burn. With twelve gallons of usable fuel and a burn rate of four gallons per hour, you could fly three hours at a stretch. The seats had absolutely no cushion.

During a checkout flight in the Aeronca Champ, instructor Gary W. Giffar told the Aviator to let go of the stick and look at him in the rear seat. The Aviator turned his head to look at Gary. Gary was holding the exposed aileron control cables in his hands, demonstrating that the airplane could be banked from the back seat without even touching the stick. The aileron control cables ran up the sides of the fuselage on either side of the rear seat.

To the Aviator, the hand prop starting procedure was exciting and nostalgic. The safe and proper way to start the engine was a two-man operation; one man at the prop and one at the controls in the cockpit. Both had to know the drill.

The Aviator gladly embraced the experience of throwing the propeller by hand as well as learning the cockpit procedure. Clear and correct communication between the pilot and the prop man was imperative. Getting out of synch with your prop man could dismember him or kill him.

The Aviator got to practice both roles. Once familiar with the procedure and checked out for solo flight, he was hankering to rack up a crap-load of stick and rudder time all by his lonesome self.

With the Aviator at the controls, Gary stood at the prop and called out the pre-start commands. The Aviator echoed each command as soon as it was completed.

"Switch off."
"Switch off."
"Throttle closed."
"Throttle closed."
"Brakes."
"Brakes."
"Contact left only."
"Contact left."

Gary threw the prop. The old, sixty-five-horse Continental four-banger sputtered to life on the first try. As soon as the engine fired, the Aviator finessed the throttle to keep the engine running. He set the magneto switch to both and checked oil pressure. Not much else to do in this airplane except enjoy it.

Alternating his head out one side of the cockpit and then the other to better see past the nose while carefully doing the typical S-curve routine commonly done while taxiing a taildragger, the Aviator taxied the Aeronca Champ to the end of the grass runway. The head-out-the-side drama was probably not necessary in the Aeronca Champ, since it had great forward visibility even for a taildragger, but it's always good to practice the S-turns. Days like this were absolutely perfect.

The Aviator flew one airplane across the state to go flying in more airplanes. Then, he would fly back across the state, go home, and drive a wheat truck and a combine for harvest, save up some extra cash, and then head out on more quests for stick and rudder time. That's the way summers are meant to be spent.

As he taxied the Aeronca Champ to the end of the grass runway, he appreciated every bump and jolt reverberating through the airframe as the wheels rolled over the unpaved ground. Little details like that made the whole experience all the more enlivening.

Heels on the brakes, stick back, throttle to 1500 rpm, magneto switch to left, then back to both, then right, then back to both. No excessive RPM drop on either mag.

Controls free and correct. Throttle back to idle. After run-up and magneto check, the Aviator commenced takeoff.

Throttle open, stick forward to bring the tail off the ground for better forward visibility. Ease back on the stick as speed picks up. Barely forty-five knots and the old airplane left the ground. It was the most natural feeling in the world.

The Aviator throttled back to about 2100 RPM for a leisurely climb to pattern altitude. The view of Western Washington and Oregon just across the river to the south was breathtaking. The greenery below, the blue above, the rush of wind past the open windows, and the rattling of the engine made the Aviator feel alert and alive.

Just flying around the pattern for touch and go landings, the Aviator enjoyed not having a radio. Landings were fun. On final approach, close the throttle and fly the airplane right down to the runway. Almost no need for an airspeed indicator. You can hear how fast or how slow you are flying.

The Aviator stuck his head out the left side of the cockpit to see along the side of the cowling, and to feel the wind in his face as he flared for a full-stall landing. His feet were active on the rudder pedals. He let the airplane settle as speed bled off.

The slipstream faded. A split second of near silence. The airframe's rattling and shaking replaced the spilt second of near silence. Classic three-point landing. The tail wheel and the main gear touched the bumpy, grass airstrip simultaneously, transmitting the wheel vibrations to the airframe. The slightly uneven terrain of the grass runway had a mild rise and dip that made rollout feel like a gentle rollercoaster ride.

The Aviator could log flight time for a mere ten dollars per hour, wet rate, in these old tailwheel airplanes. They were a blast to fly! Plus, he learned a dance he wasn't at all shy about. Instructor Gary Giffar called it the taildragger two-step. That was a name jokingly given to the technique of using quick, short jabs on the rudder pedals while taxiing a tailwheel airplane.

Tailwheel airplanes, also called conventional gear airplanes, require some concentration and anticipation during ground handling. Their center of gravity is behind the main landing gear, making them swerve easily, too easily. They sit nose high, so you can't see directly over the nose. You have to go down the taxiway making a series of gentle S-turns so you can look off to the sides of the engine cowling to see down the taxiway. The Aeronca Champ had surprisingly good visibility during ground handling. Visibility in the Taylorcraft didn't seem quite as generous, but it wasn't bad.

If you're not careful while taxiing a tailwheel airplane, you can let the airplane swerve too sharply to one side or the other, ending up in a ground loop. Not only would that be embarrassing, but it could be dangerous and expensive. To avoid such a dilemma, keep your feet moving on the rudder pedals and make quick, small jabs to start and stop desired yaw changes, and to correct unwanted yaw without overdoing it. It takes practice, but it's as fun as all get-out.

Nosewheel airplanes are much easier to taxi, because the center of gravity is in front of the main landing gear. They sit with the nose level, so you can see forward. A pilot can get spoiled flying nosewheel aircraft, at least as far as ground handling is concerned.

One weekend in late summer 1984, the Aviator had rented the old Cessna-172 from Ellensburg and had flown it to Waterville and East Wenatchee. From there, he flew to Evergreen Field in Vancouver, Washington and camped out overnight under the wing, and then spent the next day flying taildraggers until his wallet ran dry.

On at least one such excursion, he took his younger brother, Aric along. It got cold and rainy late at night. They ended up sleeping inside the airplane. They ended up staying a second night and decided to call the local bishop of The Church of Jesus Christ of Latter-day Saints to ask if there was anyone who could put them up for the night. It would have been another cold, wet night under the airplane.

The Aviator had not planned for a food budget, so a meal was beginning to sound mighty tasty. The bishop agreed to fetch the Aviator and his brother and let them stay the night in his home.

"I have a daughter. Can I trust you both?" asked the bishop, point blank.

"Yes, Sir," replied the brothers in unison.

"Are you guys going to serve full time missions?" asked the bishop, further assessing the brothers' intentions.

"Yes, Sir," they responded.

The Aviator and his brother appreciated the bishop's hospitality. The next day, the bishop's wife drove the two brothers back to Evergreen Field.

Chapter Sixteen

Now, you know we had to get to this part. The closest the Aviator ever got to asking Roxanne out on a date was when, somehow, miraculously, he happened to see Roxanne and her uber-cute friend, Siri, at Pangborn Field. The Aviator did not know in advance that the girls would be there, nor did they know in advance that the Aviator would be there. The timing couldn't have been better. It was as if some higher power had arranged it.

The girls must have been there to meet someone or to see someone off on a commercial flight at the terminal, or to pick up or drop off a package, or something of that nature; memory fades on that part.

The Aviator noticed Roxanne and Siri in the terminal building while he was entering or leaving the Flight Service Station adjacent to the terminal. He was probably getting a weather briefing or filing a flight plan or closing a flight plan, or some such business. Anyway, he pounced all over this scene.

He actually sprouted a nerve or two. Granted, the girls had stepped into his world, rather than him having to step into theirs. Being in his element, and seeing the two cutest girls he knew right there in front of him, it occurred to him to ask if they would like an airplane ride. They got excited and said yes. Robo-score!

The Aviator could barely contain himself. He mustered his poise and let the girls call their parents to ask permission. The Aviator also talked to the girls' parents himself, being the chivalrous, romantic fellow that he was.

He wanted to let the parents know his intentions with their daughters, and he wanted to get permission to fly the girls to Evergreen Field with him to camp out at the airport, and then bring them home the next day. If such permission was to be granted, he wanted to hear it straight from their parents. By the same token, if permission was to be denied, he wanted to hear that straight from the parents as well. Even though he was exceedingly exuberant and uber stoked, the chivalrous Aviator did not want any chance of accidentally kidnapping the girls due to any unintentional, or intentional, miscommunication.

With his parents there was no issue. One thing he always appreciated about his parents was how completely they trusted him. He was determined not to break their trust. They had no problem with him taking the car out of town for days at a time and leaving it parked at the Ellensburg airport while he rented an airplane and flew all over the state. They had an old pick-up truck for local use while the car was gone.

The girls' parents were reluctant to let their daughters go all the way across the state overnight, so that plan was a bust. Valiant try, though. The parents had no problem with the girls getting an airplane ride for the afternoon.

The Aviator walked the girls out to the airplane and demonstrated the preflight inspection. When he put them in the airplane, they looked at the instrument panel and Roxanne asked, "Do you know what all these gauges do?"

The Aviator grinned and replied, "Yes." His expression was somewhat akin to that scene in the 1981 Mel Gibson movie, The Road Warrior, where the gyrocopter pilot lands at the survivalist stronghold, and the Captain's girl asks him if his contraption can carry two. That was, and still is, one of the Aviator's favorite movies, by the way.

Once everyone was strapped in, the Aviator turned on the master switch, pushed the mixture full rich, primed the engine, cracked the throttle, turned the magneto switch to both, and pulled the metal T-handle that engaged the starter. This was a very old Cessna-172. The pull switch for the starter was a nostalgic touch. Kind of cool. Made him feel all old-school. Plus, the mood was romantically accentuated by the presence of the girls.

The engine turned through a few blades with a reluctant Ka-Chunk, Ka-Chunk, Ka-Chunk. The Aviator finessed the mixture and throttle while holding the starter switch engaged, and finally the engine erupted to life. Oil pressure came up to normal. That's always a good sign and one of the first things to look for immediately after starting an airplane engine.

"Wenatchee Radio, Cessna One-Six-Niner-Six-Yankee, taxi for takeoff, request winds and altimeter."

"Cessna One-Six-Niner-Six-Yankee, winds light and variable, altimeter three-zero-two-eight, active runway is Two-Niner."

"Roger, Niner-Six-Yankee."

Once airborne, the Aviator flew Roxanne and Siri over Badger Mountain and Waterville. He showed them his house from the air. He lived in Waterville at the time, in an old, three-story house on Walnut Street, behind the courthouse. After flying over Waterville, he flew them over Grand Coulee Dam.

The girls eventually got bored with the desert terrain and wheat fields. They asked if they could see the mountains, meaning the real mountains. The Aviator happily agreed and headed west, over the Columbia River, and then onward to the Cascade Mountains.

The whole experience was breathtaking in more ways than one. Thundering engine, stunning mountain terrain spread as far as the eye could see beneath a serene, azure sky laced with white cirrus clouds. And two, not just one, but two, uber foxy girls gleefully making this one of the most fun and memorable days of this young Aviator's youth.

As they flew over the Wenatchee Valley, Roxanne and Siri wanted to take turns sitting up front in the copilot's seat. They asked if they could swap seats with each other. The Aviator told them to go ahead. He could have and should have charged them a kiss each, but he was too busy flying the plane. The thought only occurred to him in retrospect. Hindsight's a real fist in the gut.

Whichever of the girls had been sitting up front crawled to the back seat, and then the other crawled up front. Soon after trading seats, the girls drifted off to sleep, lulled by the sweet drone of the engine and the warmth of the sunlight shining into the cockpit. They were adorable to behold. The paternally minded Aviator's heart warmed with tender emotion as he looked over at them. There is no greater honor in the world than to be entrusted with the care of the daughters of Eve.

The Aviator had to wake the girls so they wouldn't miss the mountains they had wanted to see. Perhaps some guys would take offense if a girl were to fall asleep during a date.

It never bothered the Aviator that the girls had fallen asleep on this momentous double date where he was the only dude. After all, this was a momentous double date where he was the only dude.

That thing about group dating being a load of crap? Well, it's all good with the Aviator as long as he's the only dude. This was the best date ever. And he didn't even have sunglasses. It just doesn't get any better than that. Stud!

Chapter Seventeen

Sometimes, small details can be signs of trouble brewing. One such case began with the dim, barley discernible glow of the generator warning light in the old beater Cessna-172, N1696Y, over the Cascade Mountains. The Aviator was en route to his favorite hangout, Evergreen Field. He had already put in a full day of flying. Daylight waned.

The Aviator was aware of the faint glow on the generator warning light, but he wondered if the glow was just residual current normally flowing to the light. The light was not actually on. It was not fully lit. It was not bright red. So, he reasoned, it was probably not indicating a generator failure.

He usually flew this airplane in broad daylight. A residual glow on a warning light would not have been noticeable at all in full daylight. Nevertheless, any unexpected glow on a warning light, no matter how faint, should be treated as a warning that something is amiss.

The Aviator made a poor judgment call by not shutting off all external lights immediately upon noticing the faint glow. He could have shut off the radios, too, and only turned them on when he needed to use them.

He continued on to Evergreen Field, landed safely in the twilight, and camped under the airplane. The next day, when he attempted to start the engine, the battery was dead. There was not enough charge left to turn the prop at all. The generator or something in the charging system had indeed failed, and the lights and radios had drained the battery en route over the mountains.

That is precisely why airplane engines have magnetos. The spark plugs do not rely on current from the battery or the generator, so even with a dead battery and a dead generator, the engine will keep running.

With the help of some of the FBO hands at Evergreen Field, the embarrassed Aviator got the problem resolved. One fellow helped the Aviator hand prop the Cessna-172. With engine running, the Aviator looked at the generator warning light. He didn't see any hint of a glow. But it was daytime, so he should not have expected to see a faint glow at this point.

He assumed the generator had merely had a glitch and was now functioning and charging the battery. He thought he could let the engine run at a fast idle for a few minutes and build enough charge for one restart.

Then, he realized his wallet was hemorrhaging greenbacks at the rate of twenty dollars per hour just letting the engine run and not actually doing anything with the airplane. The Hobbs hour meter was ticking away, draining his stick and rudder budget a lot faster than lights and radios had drained his battery. Not the way he wanted to spend his wages. He pulled the mixture and killed the engine.

He got the tow bar out of the airplane, hooked it to the nose gear, and began pulling the airplane across the flight line toward the shop. He asked if he could borrow a battery charger and get some help on repairing whatever was causing the problem in the first place. The fellow that had helped the Aviator hand prop the airplane shook his head and said, "I don't know about you."

It would have made much more sense to pull the airplane over to the shop in the first place. The Aviator could have at least taxied it to the shop after having gone to the trouble of hand propping it. The Aviator was more than a little embarrassed.

Let's face it. He was a nerd. He over thought stuff. He was in his forties when his younger brother, Aric had to explain to him at a family reunion that the expression, "crap a waiter" did not refer to a massive, waiter-size volume of fecal material deposited in a restaurant toilet after an enormous meal, but rather it meant a turd that stands up, poking out of the water, as if wading in the toilet bowl. Hence the correct expression, "crap a wader." Not waiter.

The actual expression does not use the word crap. But, since this story is supposed to be family friendly, rated PG and all, we'll take editorial liberties and substitute crap.

Everything came out all right in the end, and the Aviator still had a great time flying taildraggers. Waiting for parts delivery may have been why the Aviator and his brother had stayed that extra night and had called the bishop. That was around the time when Wally Olson gave the Aviator a checkout flight in the Piper PA-28-140 Cherokee.

The Cherokee is a nosewheel airplane, but it was the Aviator's first experience flying a low-wing aircraft. He loved the feel of the low-wing Piper compared to the high-wing Cessnas he had flown. The low-wing, cantilever design looked and felt more high performance, even though the Cherokee-140 is about as grossly underpowered as a Cessna-152.

The elevator trim crank located overhead in the old Piper Cherokee-140 was a unique touch. Kind of cool. It was a simple thrill to reach up and crank the trim while working the flight controls during takeoff and landing.

Now, here's another missed opportunity. Wally Olson would have done a check flight with the Aviator in an old Waco biplane. The Waco (pronounced like taco, and short for Weaver Aircraft Company) was a classic. It had a hand propped radial engine and open cockpit. The Aviator could have flown it for a mere forty dollars per hour. But, he was so enthralled with logging time in the Champ and Taylorcraft for ten bucks per hour, he never got around to the Waco.

That was an asinine episode of procrastination. Pass up a Waco? Forty bucks an hour? Good luck finding anyone who will give you a check flight in one of those, now. And if you can find someone willing to do it, you'll have to mortgage your house to afford it. Plus, they probably won't let you solo it unless you buy it first.

After Christ returns, the unrequited Aviator calls first dibs on every airplane he never got to fly. And he will build and test pilot his own designs. And offer free rides to girls!

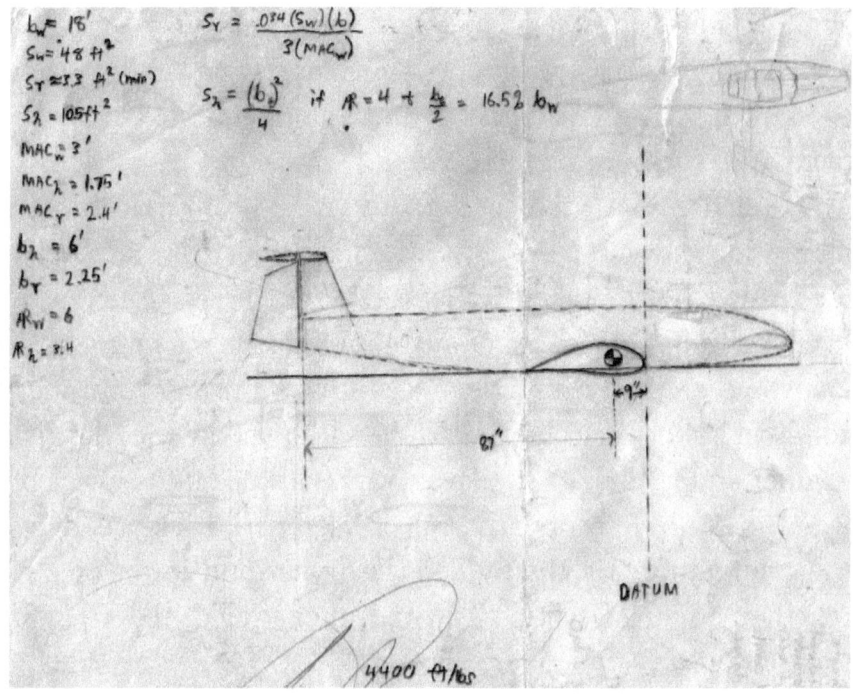

CHAPTER EIGHTEEN

In high school, Roxanne attended the Eastmont High School debate team. The Aviator had joined the debate team at Wenatchee High School. He had a chance to see her during debate tournaments.

At one tournament, the Aviator gave an expository presentation on why airplanes fly. In spite of his trepidation about public speaking, he was excited to explain how aerodynamic forces work on an airplane wing. He enjoyed explaining stall characteristics and angle of attack and load factor and such.

He had constructed a model wing structure by carefully gluing long, wooden surgical sticks together. He developed his own method warping the sticks into precise curves to fashion the upper and lower airfoil cambers for the wing ribs. He would patiently soak the sticks in warm water until they softened, and then he would bend them to the desired camber and hold them in place with pins stuck into a piece of wood or sturdy cardboard. Once dried, the sticks retained their curvature. He then glued the upper and lower curves together to form wing ribs, and then glued the ribs to the spar.

During his exposition speech, his hands shook so much from nervousness that his model wing wobbled rather comically, as if flying through severe turbulence. That embarrassed him all the more. But, he got through it.

Only once did he win an award for debate. He earned a first place trophy for being undefeated in Lincoln-Douglas debate. Lincoln-Douglas debate is a one-on-one style of debating, rather than team against team. He felt great relief and a sense of accomplishment after having faced his fear of speaking in front of a group of people. To have actually earned something tangible from the experience added another measure of satisfaction to the experience.

At one point, when he walked into the host school gymnasium where the various teams had their tables and break areas set up, he saw Roxanne. Some fellow named

Frank was giving her a shoulder massage. That was more than a little bothersome to the secretly jealous Aviator, but he politely said hello to both of them and sat somewhere else, brooding.

He had faced his fear of public speaking, but still failed to summon the courage to say, "Get your hands off my girl!" That might have actually worked if he had had the courage to make Roxanne his girl in the first place.

The Aviator never made a move. He never asked Roxanne out on a date, except for that one time when he took her and Siri flying, and that was simply because they were in the right place at the right time. He didn't have to go out of his way to arrange that date. God himself had arranged that date for him. But, the Aviator didn't take the hint. Doofus!

He was head-over-heels in love with Roxanne, the girl of his dreams, whom he had loved in his heart since he was fourteen years old more deeply than he would ever say out loud. But, he neglected her. He succumbed to his fear of rejection and his fear of losing her if he had to compete with other guys for her attention.

Well, you can guess whose fears became self fulfilling prophecies. And then, there was the lamest excuse of all, not wanting to come on too strong and impose upon her or frighten her away. Now, that was just plain stupid.

Chapter Nineteen

December 31, 1984, the Aviator rented a Cessna-172, tail number N65564 from Columbia Skyways at Pangborn Field and flew his photography teacher, Mr. Bradley, around Mount Rainier to take photos. They developed the photos in class at Waterville High School in early January 1986, when school started after Christmas break.

The photos were taken in color, but they turned out with a greenish hue. Shown here are black and white reproductions. The view was spectacular, and the photos do not do justice to the scenery. They are, however, tokens of a cherished memory of flight.

Chapter Twenty

One afternoon, on a clear, calm, spring day, back before the young Aviator had started taking flying lessons, he was visiting his friend, Hunter Moses. He and Hunter happened to look outside. It was snowing. That didn't make sense. It was way too warm for snow. Puzzled, they went outside. The snow was strange, gritty. It didn't melt. It couldn't melt. It wasn't snow.

That day was a Sunday. As they had exited the Church building earlier in the day, before going to Hunter's house, there had been an unusual, dark cloud expanding from the west toward the Wenatchee Valley. The Aviator had assumed it was a storm system, but it didn't look like what a storm cloud should look like. Even his young and inexperienced mind sensed there was something off about this cloud.

The date was May 18, 1980. Mount Saint Helens had erupted. Ash fell all over central and eastern Washington, and then some.

Three or four years later, the Aviator flew over the crater of Mount Saint Helens. He couldn't resist the urge for adventure. He flew down into the crater and circled a time or two, looking down into a spot where he could see the glow of lava in a deep crevice. Then, he made a spiraling climb out of the crater and flew on to his destination.

Years later, someone told him it was illegal to fly into the crater. Oh, well. It's not like that would have stopped him at the time. Legalities aside, the experience was one of many cherished memories.

DATE 19 84	MAKE MODEL	REG. NUMBER	FROM ↑ ↓ TO	PROCEDURES – MANEUVERS	AIRCRAFT SEL
7/7/84	C-172	N1696Y	KLN Local	A/C check Ride in CAP plane OK to use Owner A. Pellet CFI 2176567 97 Exp-2-2-85	:8
7/7/84	C-152	48868	EAT-ELN-EAT	cross country	1:0
7/8/84	C-172	4844J	EAT-PUW-EAT	cross country	3:2
7/18/84	C-172	1696Y	ELN-PUW-OKN-ELN	cross country	4:4
7/26/84	C-152	48868	EAT-KENNEWICK-EAT	cross-country	2:0
8/1/84	Beaver 7K	2583E	Vanc Local	Bis Mfalls CFI 14 2071337	1:7
8/4/84	C-172	1696Y	ELN-CHEHALIS	cross-country	1:5
			SPECIAL ENDORSEMENTS – BIENNIAL FLIGHT REVIEW – GROUND INSTRUCTION	PAGE TOTAL	14:6
				BROUGHT FORWARD	92:2
				TOTAL	106:8

	AIRCRAFT CATEGORY & CLASS		FLIGHT CONDITIONS					CROSS COUNTRY	PILOT TIME		TOTAL
	SEL	MEL	DAY	NIGHT	INSTRUMENT				DUAL	P.I.C.	
					ACTUAL	HOOD	SIMULATOR				
2-2-85	:8	:	:8	:	:	:	:	:	:8	:	:8
	1:0	:	1:0	:	:	:	:	1:0	:	1:0	1:0
	3:2	:	3:2	:	:	:	:	3:2	:	3:2	3:2
	4:4	:	4:4	:	:	:	:	4:4	:	4:4	4:4
	2:0	:	2:0	:	:	:	:	2:0	:	2:0	2:0
	1:7	:	1:7	:	:	:	:	:	1:7	:	1:7
	1:5	:	1:5	:	:	:	:	1:5	:	1:5	1:5
	14:6	:	14:6	:	:	:	:	12:1	2:5	12:1	14:6
	92:2	:	87:3	4:9	:	4:7	:	49:5	28:8	63:6	92:2
	106:8	:	101:9	4:9	:	4:7	:	61:6	31:1	75:7	106:8

118 — I. K. Lavanway — An Aviator At Heart

DATE 19__	MAKE MODEL	REG. NUMBER	FROM / TO	PROCEDURES—MANEUVERS	No. of Landings	AIRCRAFT SEL
8/4/84	C-172	1696Y	CHEHALIS → VANC.	cross-country		.8
8-5-84	ARONCA 7-AC	2583E	VANC LOCAL	LANDINGS X-WIND, CHECKOUT OK Bayard G. Fluegel CFI-IA 830-86 full stop P.I.C.		3.4
8-5-84	ARONCA 7-AC chmp	2583E	VANC Lcl	cross-wind landings & takeoffs (2) full-stop		.2
8-6-84	Tcraft	9620?	VANS Lcl	checkout Allan C129741		4
8-6-84	Taylorcraft	96202	VANS Lcl	slow flite, stalls, takeoff & landings	(7)	.9
8-6-84	C-172	1696Y	VANC - KRANEWICK	cross-country		1.5
8-6-84	C-172	1696Y	KENNEWICK - ELN	cross-country		.9
			SPECIAL ENDORSEMENTS – BIENNIAL FLIGHT REVIEW – GROUND INSTRUCTION	PAGE TOTAL		8.1
				BROUGHT FORWARD		106.8
				TOTAL		114.9

NO. of Landings	AIRCRAFT CATEGORY & CLASS		FLIGHT CONDITIONS					CROSS COUNTRY	PILOT TIME		TOTAL
	SEL	MEL	DAY	NIGHT	INSTRUMENT				DUAL	P.I.C.	
					ACTUAL	HOOD	SIMULATOR				
10	.8	:	.8	:	:	:	:	.8	:	.8	.8
	3.4	:	3.4	:	:	:	:	:	2.0	1.4	3.4
	.2	:	.2	:	:	:	:	:	:	.2	.2
(7)	4	:	4	:	:	:	:	:	4	:	4
	.9	:	.9	:	:	:	:	:	:	.9	.9
	1.5	:	1.5	:	:	:	:	1.5	:	1.5	1.5
	.9	:	.9	:	:	:	:	.9	:	.9	.9
	8.1	:	8.1	:	:	:	:	3.2	2.4	5.7	8.1
	106.8	:	101.9	4.9	:	4.7	:	61.6	31.1	75.7	106.8
	114.9	:	110.0	4.9	:	4.7	:	64.8	33.5	81.4	114.9

Chapter Twenty-One

August 4, 1984, the Aviator flew his friends, Tim and Allen Johnson, from Ellensburg to Chehalis, Washington, after which he flew from Chehalis to Vancouver, Washington, to his favorite spot, Evergreen Field. Shortly after takeoff on the flight from Ellensburg to Chehalis, the Aviator learned by experience how important it is to properly weigh and balance an airplane within specs for each and every flight, particularly when hauling a full complement of passengers and luggage. The old Cessna-172, tail number N1696Y, was loaded to the hilt, maybe slightly overgrossed, that is to say, loaded beyond maximum gross weight.

During en route climb, strong winds in the Ellensburg area must have created a downdraft on the leeward side of the hilly terrain. In spite of full power, the aircraft ceased climbing. The stall warning horn beeped intermittently. To keep airspeed up, the Aviator had to lower the nose slightly, which in these conditions meant losing altitude during the portion of his route where he should have been climbing to clear the mountainous terrain downrange.

Doing a few climbing 360-degree turns at a shallow bank is generally a good way to build altitude before crossing high terrain. However, turns mean additional load on the wings, which in this case would not result in a climb, but a more rapid descent and greater risk of stalling the wing. He continued on course.

The Aviator hoped to burn off sufficient fuel to lighten his load just enough to enable him to climb en route, or at least reach a windward portion of terrain. Fortunately, he eventually flew out of the influence of the downdraft and slowly began climbing. He was able to reach a safe altitude before crossing the mountains.

A red, helium-filled party balloon floated by, a few hundred feet below the aircraft. Nothing particularly significant about it. Just something that stuck in the Aviator's mind as a detail in the whole memory of the trip.

Kids let go of helium balloons all the time. Pilots get to see them from topside every now and then. Anyway, the Aviator delivered Tim and Allen safely to Chehalis to meet their friends or family, and then enjoyed an absolute gas racking up more stick and rudder time at Evergreen Field.

CHAPTER TWENTY-TWO

July 15, 1985, the Aviator learned first hand why it is important to shut off all portable electronic devices during flight. He was flying his younger sister, Lara and her friend, Jule Ellestad from Moscow, Idaho to Omak, Washington in the old beater Cessna-172 he had rented in Ellensburg.

He was navigating by dead reckoning. Fortunately, he was good at it. In fact, he rocked. It didn't take him long to notice the excessive discrepancy between his magnetic compass heading and his ground track.

He had a visual reference using a hill in the terrain as a landmark. It was clearly marked on his sectional chart and clearly visible out the cockpit window. The mapped terrain along the route he had plotted on his sectional chart matched what he was seeing with his own eyes out the cockpit window. Mysteriously, his magnetic compass was a whopping thirty degrees off his expected magnetic heading.

There wasn't enough wind to warrant a thirty-degree wind correction angle. Even if there were that much wind, he would have known it, because he would have had to tack the airplane into the crosswind component to hold his desired ground track. That would mean aiming the nose significantly off to one side as he progressed along his plotted route. It would have almost felt like flying sideways.

He was on course with the nose more or less pointed directly along his plotted route. Regular ten-minute position checks showed no drift. He began wondering if there was some geomagnetic anomaly in that region of Washington State.

Having an overactive imagination, the thought crossed his mind that he could be experiencing some type of Bermuda Triangle event. That would have been downright tubular! He dismissed that thought and opted to stick with contemplating more reasonable explanations for his compass malfunction. Nothing came to mind.

He couldn't figure it out, so ignored his magnetic compass and flew the course with his eyes, his sectional chart, and his clock. After a few minutes, the directional gyro was of little use. Gyroscopic precession causes a directional gyro to gradually lose accuracy unless you can reset it periodically by referencing your magnetic compass.

Suddenly, he heard a distinct click from the back seat. He noticed his magnetic compass swing back to the correct heading consistent with his ground track. He turned his head to see what had made the click sound.

Jule Ellestad was changing the cassette tape in her Walkman. When she turned it off, the magnetic compass functioned accurately. Mystery solved. He told Jule not to use her Walkman until they landed, because it was screwing with his compass.

Chapter Twenty-Three

The Aviator spent much of his youth embroiled in an internal battle between obeying rules and defying authority. In some areas of his life, he earnestly tried to abide the rules and please everybody and be impeccably and noticeably righteous in a religious way. He gradually discovered that he was, in some ways, less righteous than those who blatantly did wrong. He found that he could not judge others without condemning himself. At least other people went for what they wanted.

Okay, the Aviator went for what he wanted and took plenty of risks with airplanes. He didn't apply himself so fearlessly when romance was at stake. He did however, like to make an impression.

There was one thing he had always thought about doing. It was risky and probably illegal. He did it anyway, and he never regretted it. In retrospect, he probably would not have made a habit of it, but a one-off was a worthwhile experience. Okay, back up a second. He definitely would have made a habit of it, given the right set of circumstances.

DATE 1985	MAKE MODEL	REG. NUMBER	FROM ↑ / TO ↓	PROCEDURES — MANEUVERS		AIRCRAFT SEL
7-17-85	C-172	N65524	EAT → G-9	X-C sim Inst CFII-1657079 James W. Watson		1:3
7-31-85	C-172/RG	N6386R	EAT → EAT	OTP-sim Inst LS NDB VOR app CFII-165707 James W. Watson		1:7
7-31-85	C-172/RG	N6386R	EAT → EAT	X-C sim Inst LS NDB VOR app CFII-165707 James W. Watson		2:0
7-31-85	C-172/RG	N6386R	EAT → Lel	Steep turns, takeoffs & landings		:4
8-10-85	C-172/RG	N6386R	EAT → WHVI	x-country		:4
8-11-85	C-172/RG	N6386R	St. John → PU St. John	x-country		1:0
8-14-85	C-172/RG	N6386R	St. John → Lel	takeoffs & landings (short field)		1:8
SPECIAL ENDORSEMENTS — BIENNIAL FLIGHT REVIEW — GROUND INSTRUCTION					PAGE TOTAL	8:6
					BROUGHT FORWARD	163:6
					TOTAL	172:2

AIRCRAFT CATEGORY & CLASS		FLIGHT CONDITIONS					CROSS COUNTRY	PILOT TIME		TOTAL
SEL	MEL	DAY	NIGHT	INSTRUMENT				DUAL	P.I.C.	
				ACTUAL	HOOD	SIMULATOR				
1:3	:	:	1:3	:	1:2	:	1:3	1:3	:	1:3
1:7	:	:	1:7	:	1:6	:	1:7	1:7	:	1:7
2:0	:	:	2:0	:	1:7	:	2:0	2:0	:	2:0
:4	:	:	:4	:	:	:	:	:	:4	:4
:4	:	:	:4	:	:	:	:4	:	:4	:4
1:0	:	:	1:0	:	:	:	1:0	:	1:0	1:0
1:8	:	:	1:8	:	:	:	:	:	1:8	1:8
8:6	:	:	8:6	:	4:5	:	6:4	5:0	3:6	8:6
163:6	:	:	153:3	10:3	16:9	:	89:5	48:3	115:3	163:6
172:2	:	:	161:9	10:3	21:4	:	95:9	53:3	118:9	172:2

August 11, 1985, the Aviator embarked on a little, early morning adventure he had been planning. He had finished operating a combine for Merle Jacobsen during wheat harvest near Waterville, Washington.

Translating his harvest pay into flight time, the Aviator rented a four-seat Cessna 172RG, tail number N6386R, from Pangborn Field. The 172RG had retractable landing gear, a constant speed propeller, and a 180-horse engine, a real hot ride at that time for the eighteen-year-old Aviator on a limited budget.

Using a description of landmarks he had requested at the close of the school year, the Aviator got out his sectional chart and plotted a course to a target destination in eastern Washington. It was not an airport.

For an additional measure of accuracy, he also plotted a VOR fix by intersecting VOR radials from two different VOR stations. He would dead reckon to his target and use the VOR fix to double check his dead reckoning. He found the farm with no trouble.

The Aviator had a wonderful math and science teacher during his last year of high school. Her name was Sue Norris. Everyone affectionately called her Nora. He grew quite fond of her, and she of him.

The Aviator landed on the dirt road near the main farmhouse that was his destination near Saint John, Washington. After landing, he taxied the airplane a little way down a road perpendicular to the one on which he had landed. The place where Nora was staying was down this side road.

He killed the engine, got out and waited for a while, breathing in the cool, fresh, morning air. Then, he noticed the landing gear was beginning to sink into the soft, moist soil on the roadside.

He got back in the airplane, started the engine, and managed to taxi it back to the more solid dirt road on which he had landed. It took almost full power to get the wheels out of the mud.

He taxied the airplane back to the main farmhouse, which was Nora's parents' house. Their family name was Hollingsworth, if memory serves correctly. The house had a steep driveway going up from the road. The Aviator poured on the power and taxied the airplane straight up the driveway, parked it, shut it down, and got out.

He didn't have to wait long before Nora's parents and other relatives in the house came out to find an airplane in their driveway and a super-stoked, eighteen-year-old Aviator grinning from ear to ear.

His excuse might have been that he didn't want to wake Nora at dawn to make her drive out to an airport miles away from the farm to pick him up. Asking her to meet him at an airport would have ruined the surprise. The Aviator wanted to surprise Nora by showing up in her driveway with an airplane.

He had taken her flying before, back in Waterville. One time, he had an interesting experience with parallax while he took Nora flying above a thin layer of stratus clouds. He looked down through the thin stratus layer skimming by, just beneath the airplane. The thin layer rushing by made the ground appear to move in the opposite direction. The effect made him feel as if he were flying backward. He pointed it out to Nora.

Another time, while taking an airplane back to Pangborn Field, the Aviator flew Nora down pine canyon to the Columbia River. He loved doing low level flying down the canyon from Waterville to the river and along the river to East Wenatchee.

Nora was well aware of the Aviator's interest in airplanes. He often complained about his throttle hand getting itchy when he spent too many days outside of a cockpit. By this time, the fact that he flew airplanes was no surprise to her. The fact that he landed one in front of her parent's house unannounced and parked it in their driveway was definitely a surprise.

"Can we have a ride?" asked Nora's kinfolk.

The Aviator was more than happy to oblige. Giving airplane rides to his astonished high school teacher and her family after they awoke to find him casually relaxing beside an airplane in their driveway made their day. And his. Made his whole week!

As the Aviator prepared for takeoff with one load of passengers, a car came along the intersecting road, off the starboard wing, just behind where the Aviator began his takeoff roll. His overactive imagination kicked in as he worried about the driver getting the tail number of the airplane and calling in a complaint to the Federal Aviation Administration (FAA).

The Aviator quickly finished his run-up, cowl flaps open, mag switch to both, wing flaps twenty degrees, trim set for takeoff. Wide open throttle, brakes released. The Aviator commenced his takeoff roll before the car got too close. His intention was to obscure the view of the tail number with dust from the prop wash. It must have worked. Or the driver of the car never made an issue of it. Either way, the Aviator never caught wind of any squawking about his daring and questionably legal rural escapades.

Using the dirt road as a landing strip was a total blast. Every detail was a thrill. Gear down. The aerodynamic drag caused by the extended landing gear helps when a steep descent is needed. Cowl flaps closed for descent, to avoid shock cooling the engine at reduced power. With a full load of three passengers per flight, the Aviator flew a careful approach toward the power lines.

The power lines ran along the intersecting, perpendicular road where the car had been earlier. The power lines crossed his approach to the road on which he had committed to land, which was the road that ran in front of Nora's parents' house. He reapplied power to slow his descent as he approached the wires. Full flaps.

He could have done a slip maneuver to lose altitude without gaining too much airspeed. That would have been more effective for this particular approach. But, he did not want to alarm the passengers, who surely had no idea what a slip maneuver was. They might think the airplane was falling out of the sky on its side.

Immediately after crossing the power lines, he closed the throttle and shoved the yoke forward to drop the nose steeply toward the road. Right before impact, he firewalled the throttle and pulled back on the yoke, flaring through ground effect. The stall warning horn screamed, indicating the wing angle of attack was on the verge of critical. Exactly what he wanted, exactly when he wanted it. The mains kissed the dirt firmly. The Aviator cut the power, dumped the flaps, and stood on the brakes, opened the cowl flaps, and relished the awesomeness of a well executed landing.

"We're gonna make a bush pilot out of you yet," said Nora.

The Aviator grinned confidently, robo-stud that he was. Bush flying and agricultural spraying were two types of flying the young Aviator thought he would enjoy. Alas, he never got any closer to such occupations than landing on roads and small airstrips here and there.

Pilot Logbook

DATE 1985	MAKE MODEL	REG. NUMBER	FROM → TO	PROCEDURES—MANEUVERS
8-12-85	C-172/RG	N6886R	St. John → BAT	x-country, steep turns
8-20-85	C-172/RG	N6886R	BAT → LCL	takeoffs & landings (nite, 4), turns
8-23-85	Piper Cherokee-180	N6401J	Waterville → LCL	takeoffs & landings
8-25-85	Piper Cherokee-180	N6401J	BAT → GEG	x-country
8-25-85	Piper Cherokee-180	N6401J	GEG → BAT	x-country, takeoffs & landings, steep turns, stalls
9-21-85	C-172	78187	ARC → LCL	V-OST stalls, emergency proc, hood work taft nella CF11 567 373372 6/87
11-7-85	Piper PA28R-200	N2129T	Prescott → Local	Systems, emerg gear ext, steep turns, A+O stalls BCA southwest fld or PIC Gtenulu 1645 985 FD

SPECIAL ENDORSEMENTS – BIENNIAL FLIGHT REVIEW – GROUND INSTRUCTION
11-7-85 .5 HR Preflight + Systems Review, PA-28R-200
R. Mendu 16 45 985 FD
CAP 5-88

PAGE TOTAL
BROUGHT FORWARD
TOTAL

AIRCRAFT CATEGORY & CLASS		FLIGHT CONDITIONS					CROSS COUNTRY	PILOT TIME		TOTAL
SEL	MEL	DAY	NIGHT	INSTRUMENT				DUAL	P.I.C.	
				ACTUAL	HOOD	SIMULATOR				
1:1	:	1:1	:	:	:	:	1:1	:	1:1	1:1
:7	:	:	:7	:	:	:	:	:	:7	:7
:5	:	:5	:	:	:	:	:	:	:5	:5
1:3	:	1:3	:	:	:	:	1:3	:	1:3	1:3
2:2	:	2:2	:	:	:	:	1:6	:	2:2	2:2
:7	:	:7	:	:	:2	:	:	:7	:	:7
1:2	:	1:2	:	:	:	:	:	1:2	:	1:2
7:7	:	7:0	:7	:	:2	:	4:0	1:9	5:8	7:7
172:2	:	161:9	10:3	:	21:4	:	95:9	53:3	118:9	172:2
179:9	:	168:9	11:0	:	21:6	:	99:9	55:2	124:7	179:9

Chapter Twenty-Four

August 23, 1985, the Daling family in Waterville, Washington generously allowed the young Aviator to fly their airplane, a Piper PA-28-180 Cherokee, from Waterville to Geiger Field, Spokane Washington, to take an instrument written exam. Mr. and Mrs. Daling each had a pilot license. The Aviator asked if one of them would be willing to check him out in their airplane and then permit him to borrow it to go to Spokane for his written test.

Mrs. Daling met him at their hangar and observed him preflight the airplane. They climbed into the cockpit, the Aviator in the pilot seat and Mrs. Daling in the copilot seat.

The Aviator started the engine, checked oil pressure, and began to taxi the airplane out of the hangar. His younger brother, Ayon, had rushed out to the airport on a bicycle, hoping to get an airplane ride.

Ayon reached the hangar and skidded to a halt just as the Aviator was taxiing out of the hangar. The Aviator, being a social retard, simply waved as dust from the prop wash engulfed Ayon. The Aviator never thought to stop the airplane and invite Ayon to get in for a ride.

Surely, Ayon was disappointed about that. It was not until much later, after reflecting back on that day, that the Aviator realized how his younger brother must have felt. But it was too late.

The obtuse Aviator often missed key moments that could have been shared with others. And he has often spouted off, saying things that have offended others, perhaps for life.

Chapter Twenty-Five

Sometimes, the Aviator actually learned from his mistakes. Bear with a few background details here, before we get to the point.

March 27, 1986, while attending his freshman year at Embry-Riddle Aeronautical University's pre-engineering program in Prescott, Arizona, the Aviator got checked out in a Grumman AA-5B Tiger. He let a fellow Embry-Riddle student ride along during the flight.

The checkout flight went exceptionally well. The Aviator was quite happy about having added another airplane to his burgeoning repertoire. The Grumman Tiger was particularly fun, because it had a sliding canopy that could be fully open during ground operations, giving an open cockpit feel to the experience. The Aviator was reluctant to open the canopy in flight for fear of having his navigation charts sucked out of the cockpit. That would suck.

"I'll fly with you anytime," said the fellow student, as the Aviator taxied the airplane back to the flight line.

The Aviator often had trouble reading people. He seldom, if ever, caught hints. He had difficulty discerning whether or not a person was serious of joking. He almost got into an argument with this same well-meaning friend a few days later.

April 6, 1986, this fellow Embry-Riddle student had asked the Aviator to fly him and another friend to Phoenix, Arizona. A third student, named Jesse, wanted to ride along. It would be a full airplane with three passengers and some luggage.

The Aviator immediately recalled his experience flying Tim and Allen Johnson from Ellensburg to Chehalis nearly two years prior.

Happy to oblige, the Aviator rented a Cessna-172 and began the process of weighing and balancing the airplane. This does not mean physically parking the airplane on a scale to weigh it. The process is accomplished by using a weight and balance chart located in the airplane's Pilot Operating Handbook (POH). Add the weights of passengers and baggage and fuel to the aircraft's empty weight listed in the specifications.

The total must be less than the gross weight listed in specs. Not only is total weight on board an issue, but how that weight is distributed, how it affects aircraft center of gravity (CG) is equally important, if not more so. You might get away with flying an aircraft slightly over gross weight (don't do it), but it is extremely dangerous to have an out of tolerance CG, even if you are well under your gross weight.

If the CG is too far aft of the specified datum, the airplane may never recover from a stall, and it would be too easy to stall it since it is tail-heavy. You won't generate enough aerodynamic force on the elevators to lower the nose at low airspeeds. Landings would become extremely risky.

The weight and balance chart has an envelope, or range of tolerance limits within which the total moment and total weight must remain. This helps a pilot decide how to best distribute the weight he pans to haul, keeping the CG within safe limits. Generally, put the heaviest passenger up front, and the heaviest baggage as far forward as possible. Slightly nose-heavy is better than any tail-heavy. Tail-heavy is bad.

If you are hauling girls, you can either guess what they weigh or ask them and then add another twenty or thirty percent to whatever number they give you, because they ain't gonna tell you how much they really weigh, especially if they're fat. The passengers were all dudes, so simply asking for weights was not an issue.

With the other fellows standing around watching the operation, the Aviator tallied it all up, adding estimated baggage weight after personally hefting each bag. Then, he calculated the total moment by adding up the individual moments of each weight at its associated station, or lever arm within the airplane, which is just a fancy way of saying distance from the reference datum.

The total weight and total moment were well within limits, but this one fellow kept asking the Aviator to recalculate, suggesting the totals were out of tolerance and someone would have to stay behind. The Aviator recalculated everything again with precisely the same results, well within limits. He asked the fellow what the problem was, but the fellow just pointed at the graph randomly, without any specific explanation for his concern. The Aviator recalculated a third time, and got the same results. The fellow became more insistent that there was a problem. The Aviator began to feel slightly irritated. Then, the fellow muttered under his breath, "No, I mean we don't want Jesse riding with us."

After all that loading graph drama, the fellow was simply trying to scare Jesse out of the flight, making Jesse think the loading graph was showing an out of tolerance payload. Since Jesse was just along for the ride, it was not essential for him to be in the airplane.

The Aviator eventually talked the two fellows who needed to go to Phoenix into letting Jesse ride along. Whatever reason they had for not wanting Jesse on the flight was something just between them. The Aviator never discovered the reason for their reluctance. Anyway, the flight went well, and no major arguments erupted.

Chapter Twenty-Six

Allen Johnson, a long time family friend, was an electronics genius. He always had the latest gadgets. In 1985, it was a big deal to own a personal VHS video camera.

In late January 1985, the Aviator took Allen Johnson flying around the Wenatchee area while Allen filmed the flight from the cockpit. As of this writing, the Aviator still has that original VHS tape. Almost two decades later, he had a DVD transfer made from the tape of that flight. Optical discs last a lot longer than VHS tapes.

The highlight of the flight was one of the Aviator's favorite jaunts over a plateau that dropped sharply toward the Columbia River near the south end of town. There was an orchard on the top of the plateau.

The Aviator flew out over South Wenatchee, and then turned back toward the valley. He descended from the south and piloted the airplane low and fast, skimming the bare treetops poking out of the snow covered surface of the plateau. As he flew over the edge of the cliff, he pushed the nose down steeply and dove toward the low terrain near the river.

The slipstream howled across the wing struts as the airplane picked up speed well into the yellow arc on the airspeed indicator. The Aviator gently pulled out of the dive over the river and climbed back to an altitude more conducive to sightseeing over the valley.

Allen got airsick. Fortunately, Allen managed to hurl out the window as the Aviator flew the airplane back toward Pangborn Field. Poor guy was dry heaving on final approach to runway Two-Niner. After landing, cleanup was relatively simple. Just a matter of scrubbing frozen vomit off the starboard side of the fuselage. All caught on VHS tape.

Filming actual cockpit footage probably means nothing to you, living in the age of micro high-definition digital cameras, solid state flash memory, cloud servers, and online video venues like YouTube. But, back in the day, it was definitely awesome, totally gnarly, downright tripindicular!

Allen Johnson was an amazing friend. For several months, after the Aviator returned home from Missionary service in Argentina, Allen would go out of his way to spend time with him during a particularly rough patch in life. This must have been around 1989, before the Aviator owned a car.

Allen lived in Des Moines, Washington, at the time. That was at least a thirty-minute drive to where the Aviator was staying in Seattle. Every weekend or so, Allen would drive down to fetch the Aviator. They would go back to Allen's house for the evening, just to hang out, talk about life, and watch science-fiction movies from Allen's extensive VHS movie collection. The Aviator has always been a movie fan.

Chapter Twenty-Seven

The Aviator eventually learned by experience that the solutions to some of the exceptional dilemmas in his life could best be solved, or at least confronted, by finding or making exceptions to the rules. While some of this may have stemmed from his tendency to defy authority, don't misunderstand the point here.

In order to make exceptions to the rules, you must first learn the rules and keep the rules. And you need to discern which rules should never be bent or broken, such as certain laws of God, and which ones can be flagrantly circumvented, speaking of the laws of man.

You also need to know that careful planning and forethought and good judgment can usually save you from getting yourself into a situation that requires exceptional measures to resolve. Unfortunately, good judgment is often best acquired through experience, and experience is usually the best teacher when bad judgment is in school. When life kicks your butt, crap on its boot.

The Aviator invented exceptions to a few rules during the final leg of his longest and most adventurous cross country flight. He was flying a Piper PA-28R-200 Arrow, tail number 2129T, from Prescott, Arizona to Waterville, Washington for Christmas break.

He was in his freshman year of college at Embry-Riddle Aeronautical University, Prescott Campus, on a full scholarship from Air Force Reserve Officer Training Corps (ROTC). He had initially applied to the Air Force Academy, but had been turned down. It turns out that ROTC was the far better route, but that's a whole other story for a whole other time.

December 1985, the Aviator was giving a friend named Mike a ride from Prescott, Arizona to Moses Lake, Washington, where Mike's family lived. The four-hour, 473-mile leg from Love Field, near Prescott, Arizona, to Elko, Nevada was uneventful and enjoyable. The Aviator had a blast navigating the longest cross-country leg he had ever flown.

After filling fuel tanks and emptying bladders at the airport in Elko, Mike and the Aviator continued their trip northward. Another four-hour leg. Late in the afternoon, the eighteen-year-old Aviator piloted his craft over southeastern Washington State.

The sun was setting. Low stratus clouds blanketed and completely obscured the ground as far as the eye could see. It became obvious that if he proceeded to Moses Lake, it would be dark and the fog near the ground would get worse. He would have to declare an emergency and request an instrument approach into Moses Lake Airfield. And he would be low on fuel.

He had had some instrument training, and he grasped the general idea of how to do the instrument approach, but he was not yet rated for instrument flight, and he did not have the instrument approach plates for Moses Lake. That meant he would have to ask for radar vectoring and let the tower know he did not have approach plates. It would become immediately obvious that he did not have an instrument flight plan on file, and that he was not rated for one in the first place.

His flight plan was Visual Flight Rules (VFR) only, and he really did not want get into a tiff with any authorities when they would surely demand an explanation. More importantly, he did not want a low fuel situation exacerbated by darkness and fog obscuring the terrain. He began to feel like he was up Defecation Creek without one of those flat, wooden, manually operated propulsion systems.

The Aviator looked at Mike and said, "Find a hole. I'm going to put it down before it gets any darker." Pasco, Washington, or any airport in the Tri-Cities (Pasco, Kennewick, Richland) area, would have been a perfect alternate airport, except that the entire region was under Instrument Flight Rule (IFR) conditions, as he could see for himself from his vantage point in the air.

The Aviator had no intentions of landing in Pasco, or at any manned airport, for the same reason he did not continue on to Moses Lake. He was determined to find a hole in the fog and get the plane on the ground without any banter with tower personnel. He ended up landing nine miles northeast of Pasco. Controllers didn't really need to know that now, did they? Anyway, it was close enough to get the job done.

DATE 1985	MAKE MODEL	REG. NUMBER	FROM ↑ ↓ TO	PROCEDURES — MANEUVERS	AIRCRAFT SEL
11-7-85	Piper Arrow PA-28R-200	N2129T	PRC → LCL	takeoffs & landings	:4
11-12-85	PA-28-140 CHEROKEE	N58974	Prescott → LOCAL	NIGHT CHECK OUT - TAKE OFFS & LDGS W/ +W/O LIGHTS OK PIC PA28-140 Splinder 1645 TR CPE Night takeoffs & landings w & w/out lndg light. 4 TRIPS	:8
11-18-85	PA-28R-200 ARROW	N2129T	PRC → LCL		:5
11-22-85	PA-28-140 Cherokee	N58974	Prescott, AZ → LCL	takeoffs & landings	2:0
12-11-85	PA-28R-200 ARROW	N2129T	Prescott, AZ → LCL	turns, emerg. gr procedure, practice approach	:6
12-13-85	PA-28R-200 ARROW	N2129T	Prescott, AZ → Elko, Nevada	cross-country (473 miles non-stop)	4:0
12-15-85	PA-28R-200 ARROW	N2129T	Elko, Nevada → Paso, WA	cross country, emerg. landing	3:3
	SPECIAL ENDORSEMENTS — BIENNIAL FLIGHT REVIEW — GROUND INSTRUCTION			PAGE TOTAL	11:6
				BROUGHT FORWARD	179.9
				TOTAL	191:5

AIRCRAFT CATEGORY & CLASS			FLIGHT CONDITIONS					CROSS COUNTRY	PILOT TIME		TOTAL
SEL	MEL		DAY	NIGHT	INSTRUMENT				DUAL	P.I.C.	
					ACTUAL	HOOD	SIMULATOR				
:4	:	:	:4		:	:	:		:	:4	:4
:8	:	:		:8	:	:	:		:8	:	:8
:5	:	:		:5	:	:	:		:	:5	:5
2:0	:	:	2:0		:	:	:		:	2:0	2:0
:6	:	:	:6		:	:	:		:	:6	:6
4:0	:	:	4:0		:	:	:	4:0	:	4:0	4:0
3:3	:	:	3:3		:	:	:	3:3	:	3:3	3:3
11:6	:	:	10:8	1:3	:	:	:	7:3	:8	10:8	11:6
179.9	:	:	168:9	11:0	:	21:6	:	99.9	55:2	124:7	179.9
191:5	:	:	179:2	12:3	:	21:6	:	107:2	56:0	135:5	191:5

The Piper Arrow was the highest performance aircraft the Aviator had been able to afford to fly at that point in his life. He thoroughly enjoyed its beefy, solid feel, and its retractable landing gear, and the macho, testosterone-laden rumble of its 200-horse engine turning a wide-chord, constant speed propeller.

This was much more his style than those wimpy Cessna units he usually got stuck with during junior high and high school, when his flight instructor thought he was too young to handle a better aircraft. Never tell the Aviator he's too young to handle a better aircraft. And by the way, never tell the Aviator he's too young to be in love. Bogus!

The Aviator banked the aircraft into a smooth, 360-degree left turn, eyes scanning the low-lying stratus layer for any hint of a thinning or an opening sufficient to reveal terrain. He knew from his navigation charts and dead reckoning skills that the terrain in this area would be mostly flat, rural land near the Tri-Cities in Washington State. All he needed was a hole. He saw nothing. He prayed silently. He circled again. Still nothing.

"Do you see anything?" he asked Mike.

"No," Mike replied with worry in his voice.

The Aviator was also worried, but tried not to show it, fearing it would worry Mike even more. The Aviator knew it was his own responsibility as a pilot to stay calm and fly the aircraft. He could not afford to let fear escalate into panic.

He banked into a right turn this time, covering the same area he had covered just minutes earlier. Still nothing. Completing a right 360-degree turn back to his original northerly heading, the Aviator was about to give up on the hole-in-the-fog idea and just head onward to Moses Lake, request radar vectoring to final approach, fly the ILS, and take his licks.

Where's the fun in that? Fun aside, was there some unknown reason God wanted the Aviator to land out here on this particular day?

"There's a road down there!" Mike exclaimed.

The Aviator looked to the right, out Mike's window, and banked into another right turn to lower the starboard wing for a better view from the pilot's seat. A sense of relief swept over the Aviator. And over Mike, too.

The Aviator became totally pumped. Time for the kind of seat-of-the-pants bush flying he had always daydreamed about during so many otherwise incessantly dull moments at school and Church.

God had answered his silent prayer. There was a hole in the fog where there had been no hole just minutes ago. Not only was there a hole, but a straight, gravel county road ran north and south conveniently traversing the hole. Of course, it was not all peachy.

A row of telephone poles along the west side of the road came into view. That sucked. But the Aviator decided it was still the best option. He would just have to hug the east side of the road during flare and touchdown. He committed to set up an approach. He saw it as his only option.

There was often an amazing transformation in this shy Aviator's character, a side of him that few people witnessed unless they saw him in his own element. One of his friends, Tony Riffe, commented to that effect after the Aviator had taken him flying around the Wenatchee area, back in high school. Tony commented that he had never seen the Aviator happier and more at peace than when at the controls of an airplane.

Wise and supposedly discerning clergy, well intended as they were, often irritated the young Aviator by assuming the young Aviator lacked commitment or feared responsibility. What did they know, anyway?

In his own world, in his element, the Aviator was not shy at all. He was in control, decisive, confident, skilled, and daring. It was his territory and he owned it aggressively. He was hard-core, a total superhero, a legend in his own mind. And judging from the plethora of aviation-related comments in more than one of his junior high and high school year books, he had become a legend in the minds of others as well. So, he really had become a legend in his own time.

It was downright over-the-top awesome when girls wrote comments in his year books. The comments from guys were cool, too, but one that mattered most was when a fellow named Trace Collier wrote, "I hope you get together with RockSan [Roxanne]." What did that comment have to do with flying airplanes? Everything. At least, it did at the time. As you've undoubtedly ascertained by now, Roxanne was the love of this young Aviator's youth.

"I'm gonna put it on that road!"

The Aviator pulled back the throttle to bring the manifold pressure down a smidge, pushed the prop control full forward to flatten the blade pitch and increase RPM, pushed the mixture to full rich, hit the fuel boost pump, verified fuel pressure, oil pressure, and oil temperature all green. Once his airspeed had slowed sufficiently, he pulled the wing flap control lever to the first notch for ten degrees deflection, lowered the landing gear, and trimmed for a rapid descent.

"I'm gonna slip it to lose altitude," he told Mike. He wanted to avoid alarming Mike with an unexpected maneuver in an already stressful situation.

Descending in a right three-sixty to overfly the road for a closer look, the Aviator stood on the left rudder and cranked in more right aileron. The slipstream roared liked a demon. The vertical speed indicator pegged in descent exceeding two-thousand feet per minute. Ears hurt from pressure change. The Aviator flexed jaw and tongue to open Eustachian tubes, allowing his ears to equalize. He assumed Mike was doing the same.

Coming around through his original heading, he continued his steep, right turn back toward the road, crossing it perpendicularly on an easterly heading. After passing the road, he lay off the slip and cranked the aircraft into a steep and decisive left turn for better visibility from the pilot's seat. He craned his neck, peering over his left shoulder as he came around to pick up a visual on that black ribbon of hope traversing the gray, winter landscape in the waning daylight.

The road remained vaguely discernable through the hole in the fog. The Aviator absolutely did not want to lose sight of that road or delay his approach and let the hole close. His descending left turn circled back toward the road.

In spite of his intense concentration and the urgency of the situation, The Aviator could not help but gaze out over that vast sea of fog for a few short seconds to appreciate the brilliantly colored sunset bathing the western horizon as its deepening glow retreated westward across the top of the stratus layer.

Roxanne might have fleeted across his thoughts. No matter how the years ebbed onward, she had always been in his heart, but certain moments seemed to flood him with a surge of affection for her. By all rights, he should have brought her with him on his adventures. He always dreamed of doing so, but simply never went to fetch her.

Little did he realize, she had been waiting month after month, year after year, for the Aviator to come and get her and make her his. She might have loved him, too, but the Aviator was too blind to see it.

The Aviator piloted his craft over the road, crossing it perpendicularly on a westerly heading, this time. He lowered the wing flaps another notch for twenty-five degrees deflection while tightening his descending left turn, coming around another 270 degrees to line up with the road, heading north.

Perfect timing. The setting sun was about to drop below the horizon. Its rich, amber glow illuminated his instrument panel with a deep, clear, strangely reassuring contrast.

Beneath his apprehension about the danger and the urgency of his plight, the Aviator was secretly enjoying all this. Daylight faded ever faster as his rapid descent brought the aircraft down to skim the top of the fog layer.

As the Aviator lined up his final approach with the road, he knew he still needed to bleed off several hundred feet of altitude ricky-tic fast, or he would overshoot his intended touchdown point and barrel straight into that looming fog bank while being forced to attempt a go-around in the onset of the cold, winter twilight. In the time it would take to complete a go-around, that hole which had so miraculously and suddenly opened for him could just as quickly slam shut like the Red Sea behind Moses and the Israelites. The price of a missed approach, like the price of a missed opportunity, could be more costly than the risk of creating an opportunity where there isn't supposed to be one.

To bleed off altitude without picking up too much airspeed, The Aviator lowered the wing flaps to the full forty degrees of deflection, and then rolled the aircraft practically on its side in a left slip, cranking hard left aileron while standing on the right rudder and shoving the yoke forward. It was a dangerous maneuver to perform in an aerodynamically dirty configuration at low altitude in this airplane.

But, then again, plowing into a closing fog bank in twilight with dwindling fuel and no other landing site is flirting with a minor discrepancy as well. The Aviator had a knack for understatement. Nora had found that amusing.

Anyway, take your pick. Life isn't always about a clear choice between right and wrong, good and bad. Life is often a really bogus, totally sucky conundrum that forces you to choose the lesser of two evils, or the better of two goods. Even Adam and Eve had to choose which wrong would be less wrong, or which good would be the best good, depending on how you look at things.

Suddenly, the Aviator noticed something reassuring. The row of telephone poles that so ominously laced the west side of the road turned off toward the east, along some crossroad.

Still weary of the likelihood of close encounters with previously undetected mail boxes and road signs at precarious velocities, the Aviator set his mind on a decidedly positive contact, Navy carrier style landing. It might hurt. He just wanted to get the plane on the ground and get it stopped.

The Aviator held the plane in the slip until about fifty feet above ground level, keeping the airspeed up to allow good control and to avoid stall conditions, but not too fast. He did not want to come in too hot and overshoot the landing. He leveled the wings and lay off of the right rudder, slowing his descent to a more reasonable rate of about five-hundred feet per minute

Lined up with the road and committed to the approach, he chopped the throttle. For a split second, he reveled in that thrilling, low-pitched, throaty "Ka-Pop-Pop" retort issuing from the engine's sudden retreat from loaded rumble to idle. Probably not good for the engine, but given the circumstances, any residual thrust generated by keeping the engine loaded was not something the Aviator wanted.

With minimal flare to arrest his descent through ground effect, the Aviator perfectly executed his deliberately hard, positive contact landing, slamming the main wheels onto the county gravel with a bone-jarring thud, relaxing backpressure on the yoke just a smidge to drop the nosewheel onto the gravel, dumping the flaps and standing on the brakes, then pulling the yoke to his gut to keep more down-force on the mains to aid braking, and then kicking left rudder with some differential braking to hug the left side of the road as a signpost on the right loomed into view at eighty miles per hour, passing the signpost, kicking right rudder and a bit of differential braking to avoid going into the ditch on the left side of the road, finally slowing to a safe rollout, and taxiing gleefully into a farmer's driveway, completely unscathed, all in one fluid, masterfully orchestrated exhibition of airmanship. Yes! That positively rocked!

Such a studly rebel, indeed. If only Roxanne could have been there for this one. The momentarily not-shy Aviator was mainlining a mixture of adrenaline and testosterone in such concentrated levels that he would have surely planted a few courageous, passionate kisses right on Roxanne's adorable, pouty lips. Might have even Frenched her.

The Aviator taxied to a stop in front of the farmer's garage, shut down the avionics and external lights, ran the engine at 1500 RPM for about a minute, and then pulled the mixture to lean cut-off to kill the engine. The engine would not stop. Almost as if it shared the Aviator's surge of adrenaline and had not yet come down off it.

This was definitely not The Little Engine that Could. This was the kick-butt engine that did. It shuddered on the brink of quitting, then bucked and spit and shuddered again.

"It doesn't wanna quit", muttered the Aviator. He seriously needed to urinate. Getting impatient with a painfully full bladder, the Aviator just reached for the magneto switch and shut it off. "That'll kill it!" he said, reaching up to unlock the door latch above Mike's head.

They egressed from the cockpit, out onto the starboard wing, waddled down the trailing edge step, and planted their feet onto terra firma. Mike stooped down and kissed the ground. The Aviator just wanted to kiss a girl.

They found their own places to void their bladders beside the farmer's garage. Then, feeling relieved in more ways than one, they walked up to the farmhouse and knocked on the door. No one answered. They stood there and waited at the front porch.

Having stood upright for a while in the crisp, fresh, winter evening air after nearly four hours of flying from their last fuel stop in Elko, Nevada, the Aviator suddenly had to take a massive, emergency dump. And no one was answering the door.

Becoming quite distressed, he was about to pull a spastic heifer. He got the term "spastic heifer" from Roxanne, though he never really knew exactly what it meant. Something about a young cow going into convulsions or a seizure, perhaps. Anyway, it sounded cool, so he had to add it to his repertoire.

Snap back to the task at hand. Seriously, he was prairie dogging it, touching fabric, at this point. The tortoise was crawling out the back door. The Hindenburg was leaving the hangar. The politicians wanted to be dropped off in the oval office.

"C'mon, man! I hope they're not gone on vacation or something!" blurted the Aviator, feeling the pain of the strain while pinching back a Herculean assvalanche. "I think I'm gonna have to step around back for a sec," grunted the Aviator, eyes already scanning the yard for old shop rags or anything with which to wipe.

Then, with miraculously perfect timing, a car pulled into the driveway. Gnarly save! Never let it be said that God doesn't care about crap. After a brief explanation about the airplane in the driveway and introductions all around, Danny and Kathy Fielding were kind enough to invite the Aviator and his travel companion into their home, direct them to the much needed facilities, feed them, and let them bunk for the night.

The Aviator borrowed the Fieldings' phone to cancel his flight plan, simply stating that he was down safely in Pasco. Well, the general vicinity of Pasco, but he did not elaborate.

The next day, the fog did not lift. Weather reports mentioned a temperature inversion. Now, that just bites! Cold air settled at ground level. With warmer air above and no wind, a winter fog like this could persist for days or weeks. It did. Almost three weeks.

Mike called his parents who lived in Moses Lake, which was about a two-hour drive north-northwest from the Fieldings' house. Mike's parents drove down to fetch him the evening after the Aviator had landed on the road near the Fieldings' house. The Aviator stayed another two nights, hoping to fly on to Waterville when the fog lifted. The fog remained.

The Fieldings' neighbors, the Follansbees, who lived to the north of the Fieldings on Frontier Road, came over to visit on day two, curious about the airplane in the driveway. The Follansbees had a rather cute daughter named Cindy.

That could have been a story in itself, or at least a chapter in this story. The Aviator might have had a twinge of a crush on Cindy, but, of course, the shy Aviator made no moves. His only gesture toward Cindy was to give her a Book of Mormon almost three weeks later, when he came back to fetch the airplane after the fog finally cleared.

He never heard from Cindy again. But, whose fault was that? He never took the initiative to contact her. Then again, he had at least one other girl on his mind already.

The Aviator, being a bit socially inept, perhaps unknowingly suffering from a mild case of Asperger's disease, which, decades later he jokingly pronounced ass-purger's disease, was slow to take a hint the first night. The Fieldings offered him the use of the shower. Kathy Fielding made several comments about how the house smelled musty and rank. This was a prime example of how a nice guy can make things worse without even realizing it.

In his efforts to be polite and avoid imposing on the Fieldings, the Aviator hand washed his putrid, sweaty socks in the bathroom sink the second night of his stay. He set them to dry on the floor vent in the guest room. Two-day-old socks sitting on a vent. Nice one.

Allow me to float a clue to you other geeks and nerds out there. Washing your sweaty socks with hand soap does not kill the stench. At least ask for some bleach. Drying them on the floor vent just takes it over the top and fumigates the rest of the house with your fetid squalor. That's just plain rude, crude, lewd, and socially unacceptable.

You may not notice your own rancidity because you wallow in it and you've become acclimated to it. Those around you have not evolved to develop immunity to your vile waft. They will catch a whiff. Trust me. As a side note, if you're prone to farting in Church, like the Aviator, then sit next to a baby, or sit next to the HVAC intake vent. That way, when you rip a ripe one, people will either think it's the baby or they won't even know at all.

Three days after the Aviator landed, the fog still persisted. The Aviator called the Longhurst family who lived in Connell, Washington, not too far from where he landed, maybe an hour's drive. The Longhursts had been close friends of the Aviator's parents since he was about three years old. When the Aviator was about three years old, he and his parents and younger brother, Aric, had lived in a small, yellow house on the Longhurst farm for a short while, before moving to Wenatchee.

On day three, the Longhursts were kind enough to fetch the Aviator and bring him to their home. The Aviator waited at the Longhursts' house until later that evening, when his parents drove down to Connell to fetch him and bring him back to Waterville, where they lived at the time.

Almost three weeks later, when the fog finally cleared, the Aviator's parents drove him and his younger brother, Aric, and one of the Aviator's friends, named Neil if memory serves correctly, back to the airplane that still sat in the Fieldings' driveway, northeast of Pasco. Aric and Neil wanted to ride in the airplane on the flight back to Waterville.

Now, why was the Aviator so absent minded as to not have invited Roxanne to ride along, too? Just as well, at this point. There was something he didn't know yet.

The Aviator thanked Danny and Kathy Fielding for their continued generosity in harboring the airplane in their driveway for nearly three weeks. Finally, a clear, winter day. Calm air. Unlimited visibility.

The Aviator sauntered over to the airplane and gave it a thorough preflight inspection. He rubbed frost and ice off the wings and cockpit windows. Then, he grabbed the propeller and swung it by hand backwards a few blades to work the cold engine oil through the crankshaft and cylinders. Some might debate the effectiveness of this, but that was what he had been taught to do.

He swung the prop backwards to avoid any possibility of a sporadic magneto firing, which could be disastrous on fingers and hands. Then, he pushed the airplane back, away from the garage. He climbed into the cockpit and strapped in. He let Neil sit up front in the copilot seat while Aric sat in the back. This was Neil's first time in an airplane.

The Aviator cycled the controls through full range of motion. Elevators, ailerons, rudder, and flaps. He turned on the master switch, cracked the throttle, pushed the mixture control full rich, prop control full forward, boost pump on, checked fuel pressure and flow, pulled the mixture to lean, then boost pump off, a technique specific to this airplane.

He pumped the throttle a couple times and cracked it for start. He set the fuel selector valve to the fullest tank, set flaps twenty-five degrees, elevator trim to takeoff setting, altimeter to terrain elevation. He opened the small, side window and shouted, "Clear!"

The Aviator placed his toes on the tops of the rudder pedals to apply brake pressure. He turned the starter switch. The cold engine reluctantly cranked over with a whining thump, cough, thump, cough, thump. The Aviator counted through four blades, pushed the mixture to rich and back to lean for a few more blades, a technique often needed with this particular fuel injected engine.

He grinned with excitement and relief as the engine lit with a throaty, staccato rumble. Immediately after ignition, he pushed the mixture to rich and adjusted the throttle to idle.

The Aviator verified oil pressure, fuel pressure, and voltage. He released brake pressure, eased the throttle forward to get rolling out of the driveway. Then, he throttled back to idle as he used the rudder pedals to steer the airplane to the right, checking that there were no oncoming cars. He centered the airplane on the gravel road, set his directional gyro to match his magnetic compass, and began engine run-up procedures.

He held the brakes and advanced the throttle to 2000 RPM, cycled the prop pitch through full range of motion twice, and then turned the magneto switch to left only, verified no excessive RPM drop, then back to both, then right only, and then back to both, checked oil pressure and temperature, checked fuel pressure, and pulled the throttle back to idle.

James Follansbee had a handheld aviation radio and had offered to communicate with the Aviator prior to takeoff, to advise him of any vehicles entering the stretch of road between the Fieldings' house and the Follansbees' house. There was a slight hump in the road that made seeing traffic difficult. The radio in the airplane did not pick up a clear transmission from James Follansbee's handheld unit, but the Aviator trusted that the transmission received was an "all clear."

The Aviator eased the throttle open, glancing at the manifold pressure and tachometer as the engine thundered to 2700 RPM. The airplane accelerated down the road. At about seventy knots, the Aviator eased the yoke back and the plane smoothly left the ground. The Aviator held a shallow climb on takeoff heading.

Without hesitation, he began cleaning up the airplane. He moved the gear selector switch up to retract the landing gear. With the gear up, the airplane handled more smoothly. At about one-hundred feet above ground level, the Aviator eased the flaps up, letting airspeed build, holding a straight course along the road. He pushed the nose down a bit to level off his climb and pick up airspeed to slightly over one-hundred knots.

A bit of hot dogging was imminent at this point. Youthful adrenaline and all. Cold, crisp, dense, winter air was just begging for it. Airplanes love that kind of air.

He stomped on the left rudder while cranking hard left aileron and pulling hard on the yoke. The Aviator held the airplane in a ninety-degree left bank, pulling slightly more than three Gs and bleeding off altitude down to treetop level.

"Crank it!" exclaimed Aric.

"Whoa! What's happening?! I've never been in a plane before!" protested Neil.

"Oh, yeah. Sorry, Dude. I forgot for a sec. Couldn't resist," replied the Aviator.

The Aviator leveled the wings a bit, gained some altitude, and then came around again to buzz the Fieldings' house, wagging his wings. After the gratuitous flyby, he reduced manifold pressure to about twenty-four inches of mercury and eased the prop control back for 2400 RPM. He climbed to about 2500 feet, and headed southwest to Pasco for fuel.

160   *I. K. Lavanway — An Aviator At Heart*

DATE 1986	MAKE MODEL	REG. NUMBER	FROM → TO	PROCEDURES – MANEUVERS	AIRCRAFT SEL
1-1-86	Piper AA28-200R Arrow	2129T	Pasco Wash → Waterville Wash	cross-country, steep turns	1:9
3-27-86	Grumman Tiger AA-5B	N4525N	Prescott AZ → Local	VOR intrcpt, stalls takeoffs & landings (Aircraft – check out)	:7
4-4-86	Piper PA-28R-200	N2129T	Prescott → Local	BFR – ALL A. MANUEVERS – EMERG PROCEDURES DETAILS onfile AT CFR Ofneely 1641793CFI	1:0
4-6-86	Cessna 172	N79157	Prescott AZ → Phoenix AZ	X-country, cross wind landings	2:3
4-9-86	Grumman AA-5B tiger	N4525N	Prescott AZ → LCl	takeoffs & landings cross wind & soft field	:8
4-23-86	Grumman AA-5B tiger	N4525N	Prescott, AZ → Phoenix AZ	cross country – cross wind landings	2:2
8-9-86	Cessna 150	N17060	Inchallam Wa → Waterville Wa	cross country	1:0

SPECIAL ENDORSEMENTS – BIENNIAL FLIGHT REVIEW – GROUND INSTRUCTION

4-4-86 1.0 HR OFFL FOR BFR R.Neeley 1641793CFI 5-86

Biennial Flight Review satisfactorily completed in accordance with FAR 61.57(a)
Date 4-4-86 Name R.Neeley
Cert. # 1641793CFI Exp. 5-86

PAGE TOTAL	9:9
BROUGHT FORWARD	191:5
TOTAL	201:4

AIRCRAFT CATEGORY & CLASS		FLIGHT CONDITIONS					CROSS COUNTRY	PILOT TIME		TOTAL
SEL	MEL	DAY	NIGHT	INSTRUMENT				DUAL	P.I.C.	
				ACTUAL	HOOD	SIMULATOR				
1:9	:	1:9		:	:	:	1:7	:	1:9	1:9
:7	:	:7		:	:	:		:7	:	:7
1:0	:	1:0		:	:	:		1:0	:	1:0
2:3	:	2:3		:	:	:	2:3	:	2:3	2:3
:8	:	:8		:	:	:		:	:8	:8
2:2	:	2:2		:	:	:	2:2	:	2:2	2:2
1:0	:	1:0		:	:	:	1:0	:	1:0	1:0
9:9	:	9:9		:	:	:	7:2	1:7	8:2	9:9
191:5	:	189:2	12:3	:	21:6	:	107:2	56:0	135:5	191:5
201:4	:	189:1	12:3	:	21:6	:	114:4	57:7	143:7	201:4

After landing in Pasco, Aric and Neil walked around the airport while the Aviator fueled up, got weather briefings, computed heading and wind correction angles from winds aloft reports, and filed a flight plan to Waterville.

Aric and Neil got turned around, somehow. They wandered into a restricted area. A security guard asked what they were doing. They explained that they were just trying to get back to their plane. The guard asked them for the airplane's tail number. Aric and Neil could not recall what it was. Aric told him something like, "It has a Tango in it." The guard eventually saw to it that they made their way back to the plane without incident.

Leaving Pasco, the Aviator flew them to Pangborn Field to drop off Neil. Making a straight-in approach to runway Two-Niner, the Aviator configured for landing. As he flew the Piper Arrow down to the runway, he had plenty of room for a long rollout, so he decided to grease it down and demonstrate his awesomely cool smoothness. He made a power-on approach, which is the way it is supposed to be done in a Piper Arrow, holding about 1500 RPM to avoid shock cooling the engine during descent.

Over the threshold, he stayed on the throttle for a smooth and gradual flare. The mains kissed the runway so gently you couldn't feel the contact. Just the muffled vibrations of the wheels as they rolled along the slick, icy tarmac.

The Aviator chopped the throttle and smirked with an Elvis-like half smile curling the left side of his mouth. Rounding out the thrill of a perfect landing was that throaty "Ka-Pop-Pop" as the engine unloaded to idle.

"You greased it!" Aric shouted excitedly from the back seat. Aric was so impressed, he began clapping. The Aviator always revered his brother, Aric, with great appreciation. Aric's hearty compliment made his day. Made his whole week!

To test the slickness of the runway surface, the Aviator applied brakes for a moment. Sure enough, it was icy. The airplane began sliding until the Aviator released brakes and just let it roll until it slowed enough to turn safely onto a taxiway.

"Wenatchee Radio, Piper Two-One-Two-Niner-Tango, down and clear." The Aviator was back on his old stomping grounds.

After dropping off Neil, the Aviator flew Aric on to Waterville, where home was at the time. The airplane was lighter with only two souls on board and partial fuel. That, coupled with dense winter air, afforded a thrilling, mash-you-back-in-your-seat acceleration during takeoff.

Back home, things had already changed. The visit home from college would prove challenging on several fronts.

The miracles worked by God during this entire adventure are cause for grateful consideration. In retrospect, some thirty years after the fact, the only explanation for things working out the way they did is divine intervention.

Careful scrutiny of Google maps of the area about nine miles northeast of Pasco, Washington, along with a telephone conversation with James Follansbee on November 30, 2013, verifying the accuracy of some memories, make it perfectly clear that God had his hand in all of this.

James Follansbee still lives in that area, as of the time of this writing. On the telephone Mr. Follansbee reminisced, "You picked the perfect spot to land."

Even back in December 1985, there were power poles and power lines along Frontier Road, running southward from a point about 2000 feet south of the Fieldings' house, and running northward starting at the Follansbees' house. The stretch of Frontier Road between the point 2000 feet south of the Fieldings' house and the intersection of East Sagemoor Road, where the Follansbees' house was located, had no power lines.

The fact that a hole in the fog had opened precisely over this stretch of road at precisely the time the Aviator needed a hole through which to see, and a road on which to land, cannot be mere coincidence. The fact that there was just enough room to land a Piper PA-28R-200 Arrow after clearing the power lines south of the Fieldings' house, with room left over to slow to a safe taxi speed and conveniently find the Fieldings' driveway, opposite the intersection of Crestloch Road, cannot be mere coincidence. And their driveway just happened to be unobstructed and wide enough to accommodate an airplane.

The fact that upon landing and upon departure there were no vehicles on Frontier Road to interfere with landing or takeoff is another convenient set of miracles. Likely, there are many more miracles in all of this that remain unacknowledged to this day, but are recorded in the accounts of the angels that saw to this young Aviator's preservation.

Chapter Twenty-Eight

Now, just so you don't go thinking super-studs never make mistakes, it must be told that the Aviator certainly made his own mistakes.

During the first week of January 1986, as the Aviator prepared to fly the Piper Arrow out of Waterville, Washington and back to Prescott, Arizona, the starter's Bendix gear would not engage. The starter motor simply spun and whined. Ice must have built up in the Bendix assembly while the airplane sat outside at the Waterville airport.

The resourceful Aviator decided to improvise. He had flown old taildraggers at Evergreen Field, near Vancouver, Washington a few times to rack up cheap flight time and experience a wider range of aircraft. Those old taildraggers had to be hand propped. They had no starters.

Since the Aviator knew how to hand prop an airplane, he decided to circumvent the frozen starter problem on the Piper Arrow. He turned on the master switch, set the parking brake, pushed mixture rich, turned on the fuel boost pump, and cracked the throttle, being particularly careful to tighten the throttle friction. Then, he set the magneto switch to left only.

Left magneto was typically installed with retarded timing to prevent the possibility of firing too soon and rapidly spinning the crankshaft backwards, damaging the engine. It had the added benefit of not kicking the prop backwards into your hands and fingers.

The Aviator got out of the cockpit, walked around to the front of the airplane, and grabbed the propeller blade with his fingertips. He stood up close, chest against the propeller, so that when he pulled the blade downward, his body would be stepping backward, away from the propeller. This was standard technique for hand propping.

Given the cold, winter day, and the fact that the aircraft had sat outside for a few days, it was unlikely that this aircraft could be started by hand propping. At least one older, more experienced pilot had later commented that it was impossible to hand prop a Piper Arrow, not to mention extremely dangerous, considering it was a nosewheel aircraft with a 200-horsepower, high-compression engine.

The orientation of the propeller arc with the ground is not conducive to the safe hand propping of nosewheel aircraft in general. Never tell the Aviator something is impossible. But, there is such a thing as being too good for your own good, as the Aviator was about to discover.

The Aviator swung the propeller blade with a strong, swift pull, back-stepping in perfect, fluid motion. To his surprise, the engine fired without hesitation, and did not die. Even more surprising, neither did he.

One pull. He hand propped a Piper Arrow in the dead of winter and successfully started it on the first attempt. Legendary! But, that mattered little in light of what happened next.

The exact cause remains a mystery. The Aviator's first thought was that engine vibrations must have loosened the throttle friction and advanced the throttle. A more likely cause was that the engine got over primed during the longer than normal time between turning on the boost pump and hand propping the engine. Probably also had something to do with the fact that he left the mixture rich. Whatever the case, the engine powered beyond idle and the airplane began moving itself forward.

The parking brake was ineffective. Wheel chocks would have been useless, too. Slick, compacted snow and ice covered the flight line. The wheels slid just as easily as if they were rolling.

The whole scene was like something right out of a Stephen King movie. The Aviator initially attempted to counter the airplane's forward movement by pushing his chest against the starboard wing, planning to duck under the wing and come up behind it, climb into the cockpit and grab the throttle.

The airplane accelerated. The Aviator quickly realized that his attempt to slow it and duck under was futile. If he were to duck under the wing, the starboard main wheel might run him over. So, he ran around the wingtip and got behind it and began chasing the airplane across the flight line. The snow and ice compounded the less than ideal safety conditions. Trying to run without slipping only slowed him down while nothing slowed the airplane.

At this point, it must have been downright comical in a pathetic sort of way. The airplane accelerated faster than the Aviator could run. He was chasing the airplane, sprinting frantically across the snow-covered flight line, shouting desperately for God to intervene.

The airplane kept on going straight across the taxiway and plowed into a snow bank. Its hasty attempt at autonomy ended abruptly with a white burst of snow and a loud, muffled thud. Dead silence. Except for the Aviator's pounding heartbeat. Sadly, this time it was not a girl making his heart pound.

The Aviator stopped running and walked up to the airplane. He reached in and shut off the boost pump, the master switch, and the magneto switch. Then, he pulled the mixture and closed the throttle.

He checked to be sure there was no fire and no fuel spill or oil leaks. The aircraft was equipped with a small, onboard extinguisher. Fortunately, nothing seemed to be leaking or burning. He closed the cockpit door and walked back to the airport shop to make the most embarrassing set of phone calls he had ever had to make in his entire life.

That whole week sucked beyond all comprehension. The prop was bent. The nosewheel had folded, practically sheered off. The engine crankshaft had to be Magnaflux tested for fractures.

The Aviator's act of poor judgment brought him what seemed a lifetime of unpleasant lectures and embarrassment that defied description. His costly error burdened his kind-hearted, forgiving, and generous mother with a three-thousand dollar loan that she acquired during a time of financial distress to compensate the aircraft owner for the repair bill. The owner was understandably adamant about being compensated promptly in one lump sum. A monthly payment plan was out of the question.

The Aviator desperately tried to look at the bright side of things, or create a bright side in the absence of one. The cool part was that he didn't even die. Plus, he proved you can indeed hand prop a Piper Arrow. Just have somebody man the throttle and the mixture and the boost pump.

No. Don't try it. You could actually be killed. Nosewheel aircraft do not sit at an angle conducive to safe hand propping. The Piper Arrow's fuel injected engine has a unique starting procedure that is even more non-conducive to hand propping.

With tailwheel airplanes, hand propping is usually not a problem. The propeller disk is canted such that when hand propping a tailwheel aircraft, your body can naturally move backward, away from the propeller, as you pull downward on the blade. The nose-high configuration of tailwheel airplanes is inherently conducive to hand propping. Not sure if that was ever intentional, but it is one advantage of conventional gear airplanes.

Not so in a nosewheel airplane. In a nosewheel airplane, the propeller disk is more or less perpendicular to the ground. That means you will have a tendency to lean your body forward, toward the propeller arc, in order to get the propeller to turn enough to start the engine. Even if you are properly stepping backward, you may be leaning precariously forward as your hands try to keep their grip on the descending blade. Talk about putting your head on the chopping block. Not worth the risk. This Aviator was fortunate enough to live to tell this story, but he will never try that stunt again. Okay, never say never.

The winter bus ride from Wenatchee, Washington back to Prescott, Arizona was long and filled with dread. Hard lessons learned and deservedly broken pride occupied the portions of the Aviator's mind and heart that should have been graced with fond memories and exciting plans.

The Aviator was not looking forward to reporting back to the FBO where he had rented the Piper Arrow. But, life did go on, and the resilient Aviator had many blessings to count. Being alive to tell this story is no small blessing.

Chapter Twenty-Nine

Perhaps you've been wondering what ever happened between the Aviator and Roxanne. Nothing. During Christmas break 1985, the Aviator had a chance to see Roxanne's mother who worked in the office at Wenatchee High School at that time. He asked about Roxanne.

"She's married, living in Idaho," her mother said. That was that.

Twenty-one years too late, a flattering and previously unknown tidbit surfaced. Remember that flight in late summer 1984 during which the Aviator had taken Roxanne and Siri over the Cascade Mountains? Unbeknown to the Aviator, Roxanne had never forgotten it either. One Sunday in 2005, Roxanne happened to cross paths with the Aviator's Mom at Church.

Roxanne mentioned that she always remembered that time when he took her up in an airplane. Roxanne expressed that she had had more fun on that date than on any other date she had ever been on in her life. She also told the Aviator's Mom, "I kept waiting for him to ask me out, but he never did."

Roxanne had gotten married the year following that memorable flight. She married in 1985, the year both she and the Aviator graduated from high school. The Aviator had no idea she had married until he talked to her mom during that Christmas break. How's that for falling out of touch and missing the boat!

The Aviator had enjoyed a spectacularly memorable date, exactly the kind of date he had so often previously daydreamed about. He had let slip away the very girl he had wanted so dearly at the time, all because he had been too shy, too scared, and too slow to act.

Let that be a lesson for you youngsters out there, or anyone else for that matter, who might be reading this true life drama. Snoozers lose. Nice guys only get the girl if they take the initiative and stay persistent.

And then we have the quintessential lesson. Pride gets neutralized sooner or later, no matter how good you think you are, or how old you get, or how experienced you become. Trust me. Pride falls. No exceptions.

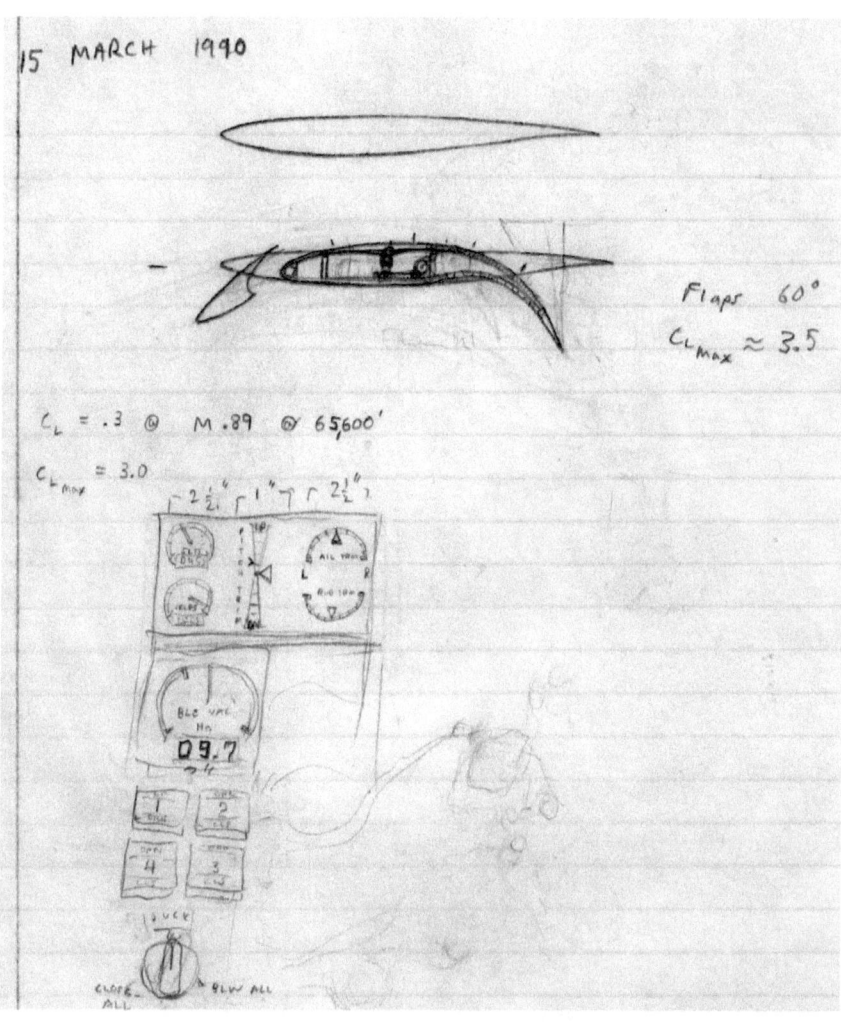

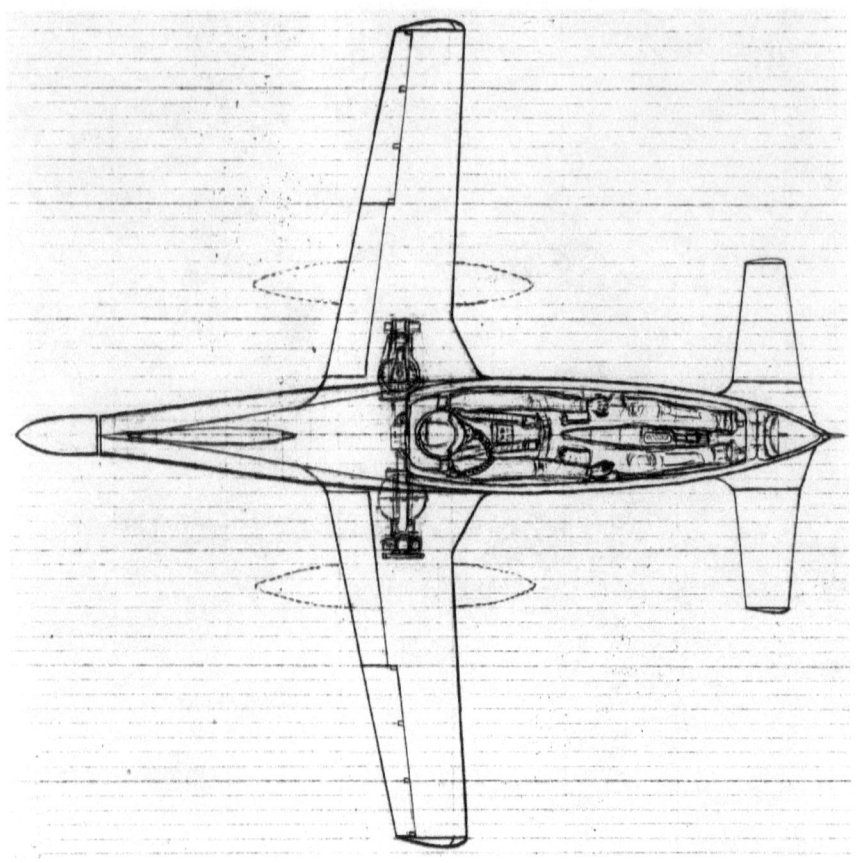

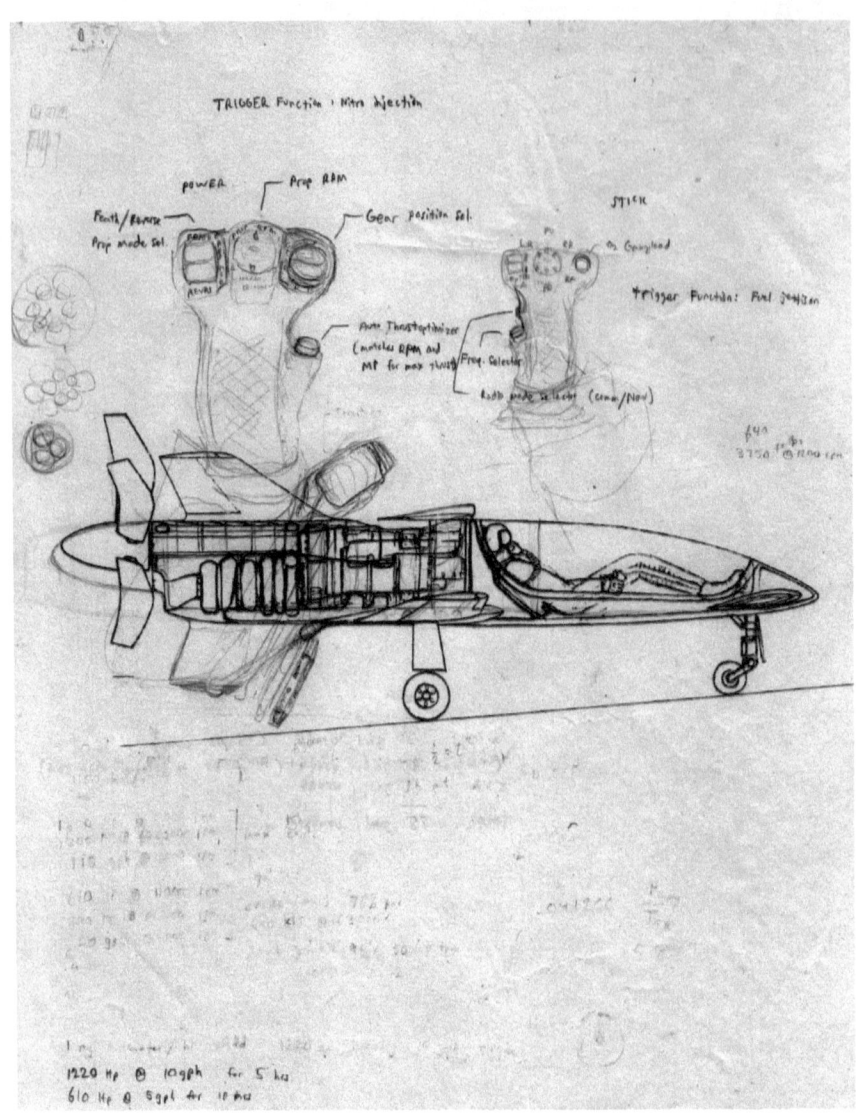

Chapter Thirty

July 26, 1991 was a momentous and long awaited day. The Aviator satisfactorily completed his instrument rating flight check with John Kell at Boeing Field, Seattle. He had studied hard, ate, drank, and slept aviation for the better part of his life, and achieved what he had set out to achieve, up to that point anyway.

Financial constraints and other life responsibilities and complications began to heap upon him. Some by his own mistakes, others simply because adversity is inherent to mortal life. Bringing to fruition unrequited dreams of his teenage years became increasingly difficult.

After returning from missionary service in Argentina, the lonely Aviator transferred from Embry-Riddle Aeronautical University's Prescott Campus to the University of Washington. Room and board were too expensive out of state. He lived with his Dad in Seattle and Bremerton for a few months in late 1988 and early 1989, and then moved to his Grandma Rosetta Harwell LaVanway's basement. He lived in Grandma's basement until early 1990.

Many a night, he would lie awake, diligently completing differential equations homework and other challenging university assignments, and his absence from the cockpit. The frustrated Aviator articulated to God his fervent determination to return to flight and complete his instrument rating.

Staring up at the floor joists above his bed in Grandma's basement, he would often mutter aloud, in Spanish, "Voy a #&^%ing volar!" Translated to English, that means "I will #&^%ing fly!" And he did not express garbled symbols. Those are editorial substitutions applied here for the sake of the easily offended.

The resolute Aviator moved locally a few times while attending the University of Washington. He spent some months in an apartment near downtown Seattle. He spent a few months in a one-room studio apartment near Boeing Field. Rent there was only 215 dollars per month.

Around 1991, he became a Certified Nurse Assistant (CNA) and worked almost a year at a geriatric care facility, called Branch Villa, in Seattle. Through his experience as a CNA, he eventually became a live-in caregiver in West Seattle for a twenty-seven-year-old Down's syndrome fellow named David Bishop. During that challenging experience, the Aviator occasionally thought to himself: *I wonder if God is preparing me for something. Perhaps I am going to have a Down's syndrome child someday.*

Before becoming a CNA, the Aviator procured employment at a campus restaurant called Arnold's on the Ave., in the University District. He flipped burgers, cleaned, opened and closed the restaurant, and was promoted to assistant manager, or the equivalent thereof. Coworkers commented that he had become a one-man show.

His job at Arnold's afforded him some much needed cockpit time. He would stand at the counter beneath the dim lights, impervious the booming music, the din of conversation, and the incessant clamor of pin-ball machines, holding fast to his self-imposed duty to study for his instrument rating during slow periods.

Studying for his instrument rating, working at Arnold's, attending University full time, as well as keeping up with the demands of Air Force ROTC and going to the temple every Saturday morning at the crack of dawn with Bishop Little of the University Singles Ward of The Church of Jesus Christ of Latter-day Saints left the do-it-all Aviator a mere four hours of sleep each night. Back then, he could handle it. After all, he was a one-man show, and there was not a more determined soul upon the face of the earth.

Sadly, as of this writing, the last time the Aviator piloted an airplane was July 26, 1991, when he passed his instrument rating check flight, administered by John Kell at Boeing Field. But, then again, life is not over yet.

180   I. K. Lavanway — An Aviator At Heart

Chapter Thirty-One

The Aviator eventually married his pen pal, a cute little girl from the Philippines who made his heart palpitate even more than airplanes did, and more than any other girl ever did. Her name is Babygirl Menchie Javellana Lavanway. That's a whole other story for a whole other time. Suffice it to say they have been married for almost fourteen years as of the time of this writing, and they have a wonderful, energetic son named Immanuel Iron Lavanway. He has Down's syndrome.

During the seemingly interminable hiatus from the cockpit, the anachronistic, still young-at-heart Aviator learned that the best substitute for the thrill of flying airplanes is doing vicarious work in the temples of The Church of Jesus Christ of Latter-day Saints.

If you want to become good at something, if you want to stay good at something, and if you feel inclined to exercise your mind and fill your soul, then serve in the temple. Ask to become a temple worker. You'll never regret it.

Generally, it is a sin to aspire to callings in the Church. Callings are issued by revelation through those in positions to extend callings. In other words, it is inappropriate to volunteer for a calling. However, there are a few exceptions. You can take the initiative to ask to become a temple worker without fear of aspiring to the call. In fact, people are encouraged to step forward and ask to become temple workers. There are not enough of them. Take advantage of that open opportunity.

Eternal and indescribable spiritual blessings aside, the attention to detail, the exactness, the precision timing, the situational awareness, the strict operations security (opsec), and the level of personal responsibility and accountability required in accomplishing temple work rival the best flight training you will ever receive. Temple work rivals the best military training in the world, and you don't even get yelled at. It is the ideal training foundation for any endeavor you may pursue in your life. In many ways, temple work is the most transferable skill set you will ever acquire.

Postface

The story you just finished reading is a true story. It is my story. I am that young Aviator. Of course, I'm a lot older, now. While writing this book, I felt the vitality of my youth return, at least in my mind and heart. That helped me keep writing.

I look forward to the day when I can resume flying. That day continues to elude me. Indeed, it seems to reside beyond the horizon of a distant future. Perhaps I'll have to wait until I'm resurrected. Either way, life is not over.

I wrote this story for posterity. Much has been said of the importance of getting to know our forefathers through searching whatever records of their lives are obtainable. I am not yet well practiced in searching the records of my forefathers. However, I am somebody's forefather. I thought I might make it easier for my posterity, and anyone else interested, to learn something of my history expressed in the form of a story.

Okay, some of you will take it as a lame, boastful, conceited, and perhaps blatantly narcissistic attempt at self validation and self promotion. Anytime a guy sticks his neck out by telling his own story in the third person, he's asking for it. There will always be more critics than fans. That's no reason to give up. Of course, you're entitled to your opinions. So am I.

This story projects, at least in part, how I saw myself in my youth. It also reflects how I desired to be seen in my youth. It is an account of my memories expressed as accurately as I can recall them. Many of these memories are indelibly forged into my mind. I quoted dialogue as closely as possible to the actual words spoken. In the event that I could not completely recall what was said, I expressed what would have been typical in the given situation.

For illustrations, I included several sketches that I drew during my youth. They are but a few of many. I also included several photos taken during my younger days. Aside from adding some personal visual context to the story, the images may serve to authenticate the story.

###

Aircraft Flown

The following is a list of aircraft I have piloted at one time or another between 1983 and 1991, inclusive. This list is not in chronological order:

Cessna-150
Cessna-152
Cessna-172
Cessna-172RG
Aeronca 7AC Champ
Taylorcraft BC-12D
Grumman AA-5B Tiger
Piper PA-28-140 Cherokee
Piper PA-28-151 Warrior
Piper PA-28-180 Cherokee
Piper PA-28R-200 Arrow

My younger brother, Aric Ramon Lavanway, ever the jovial humorist, taped this comic strip to the back of my pilot logbook, around April 1984. It is still there as of the time of this writing. It reads:
"Here's my flight plan with my E.D."
"E.D.? Oh...Estimated Time of Departure?"
"No...Estimated Destination."

SKETCHES

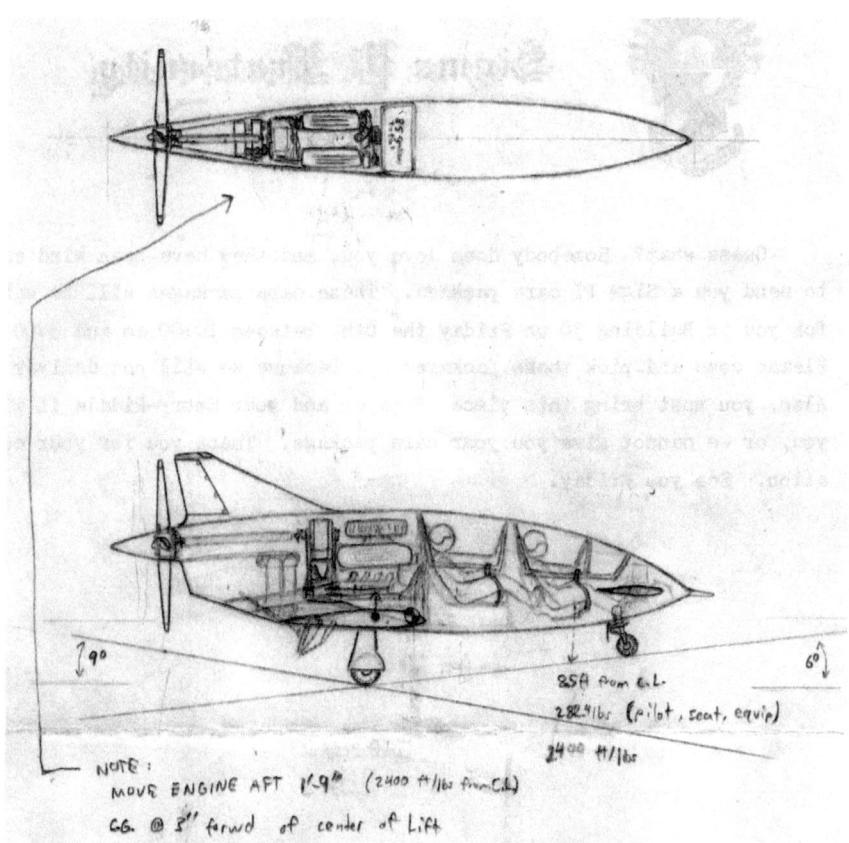

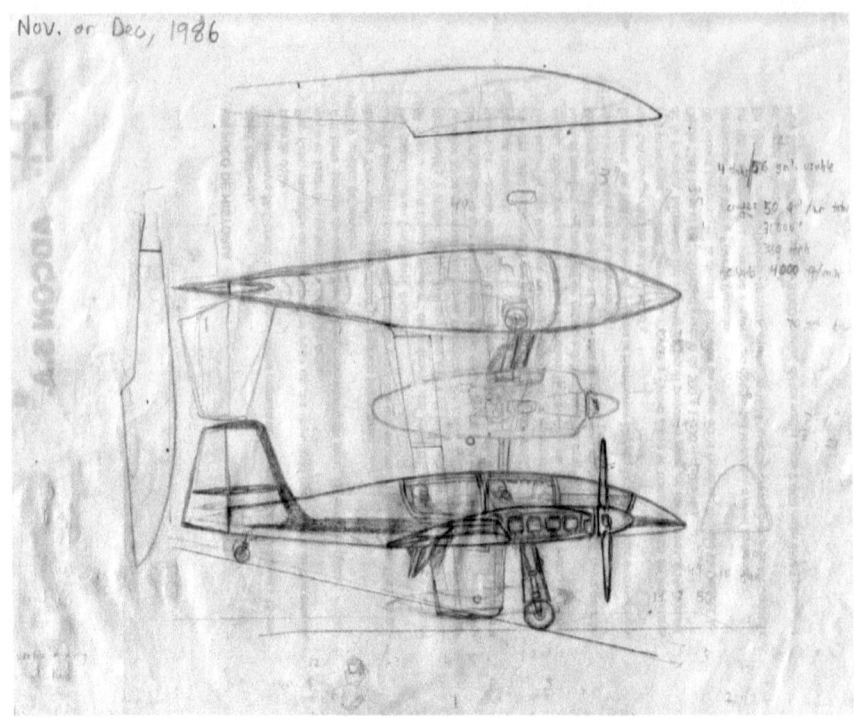

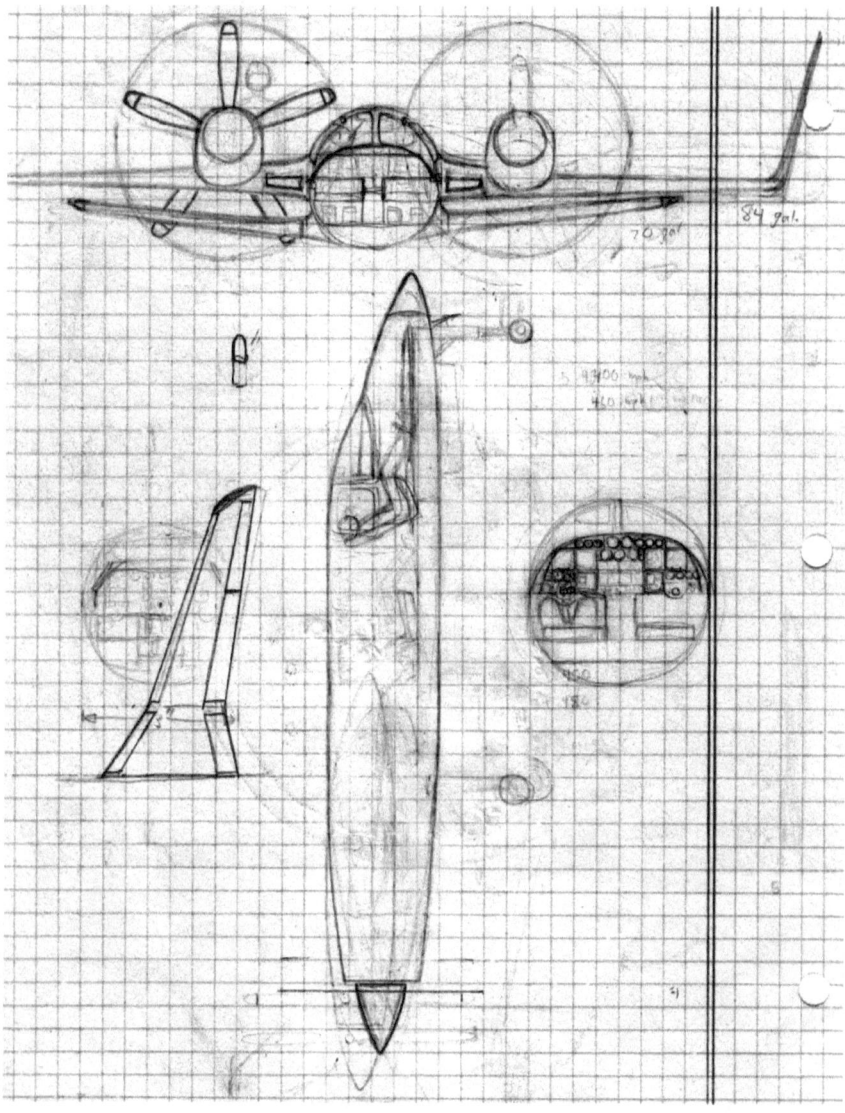

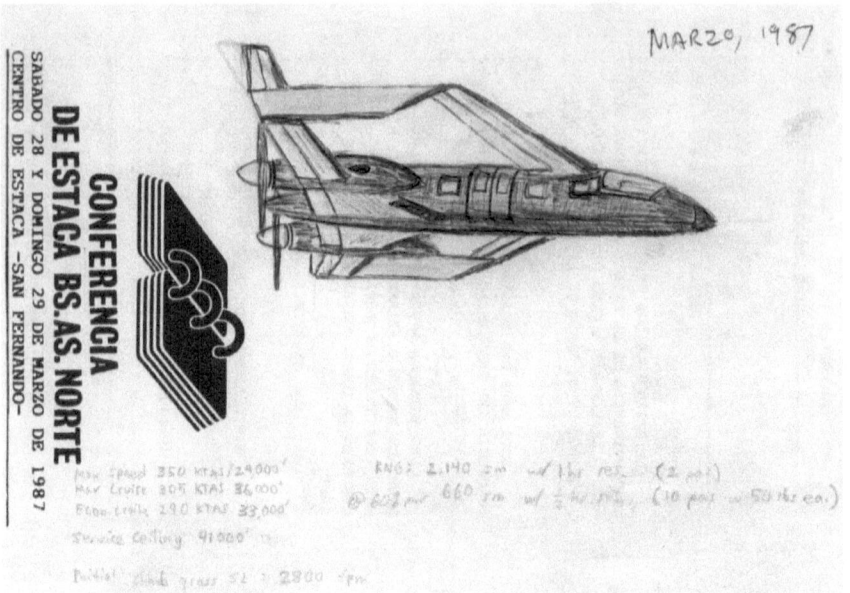

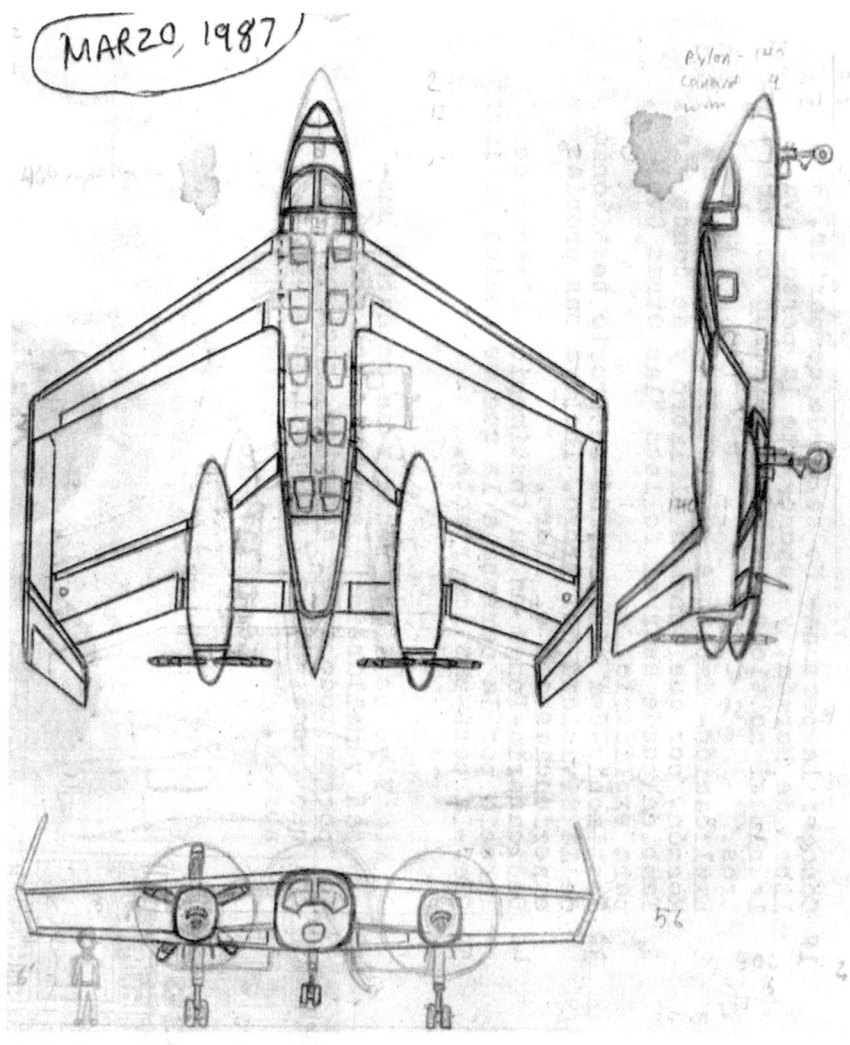

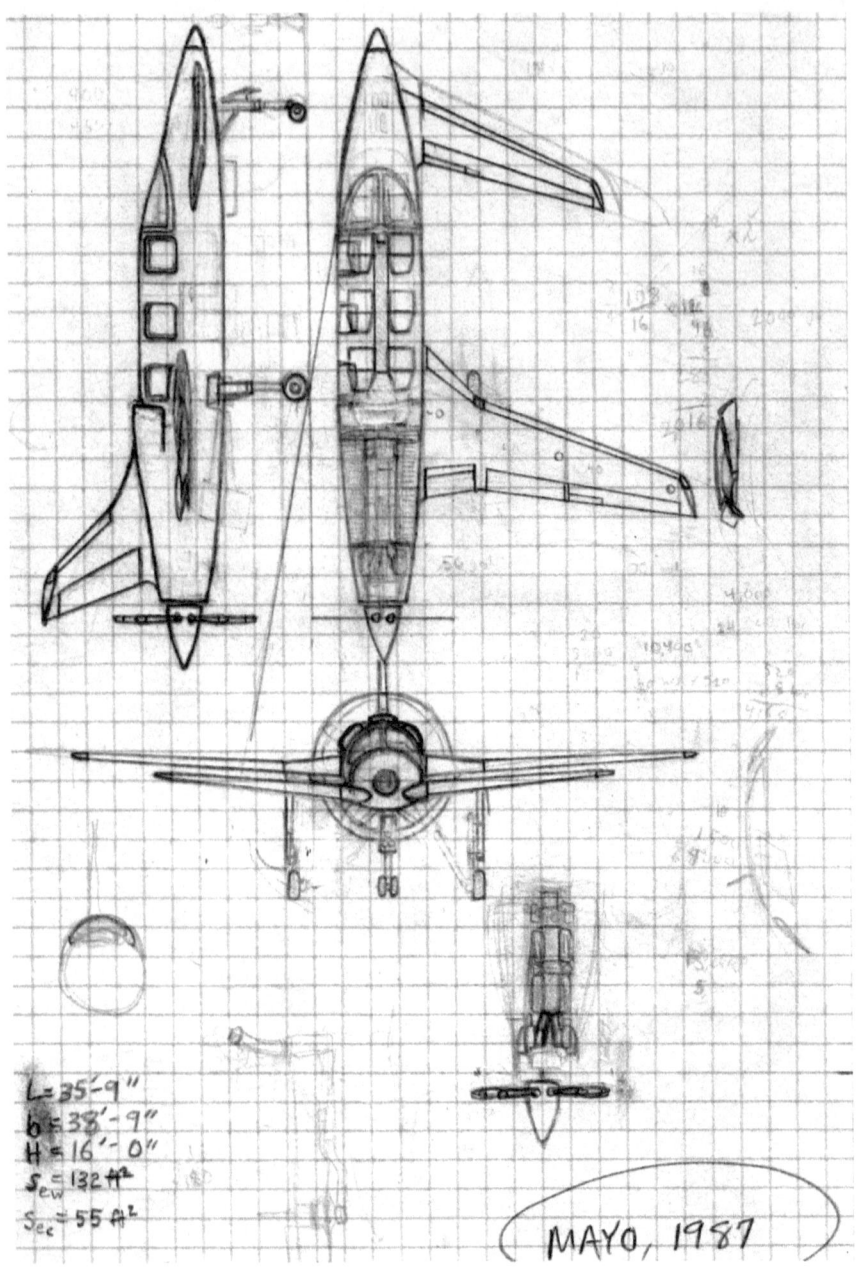

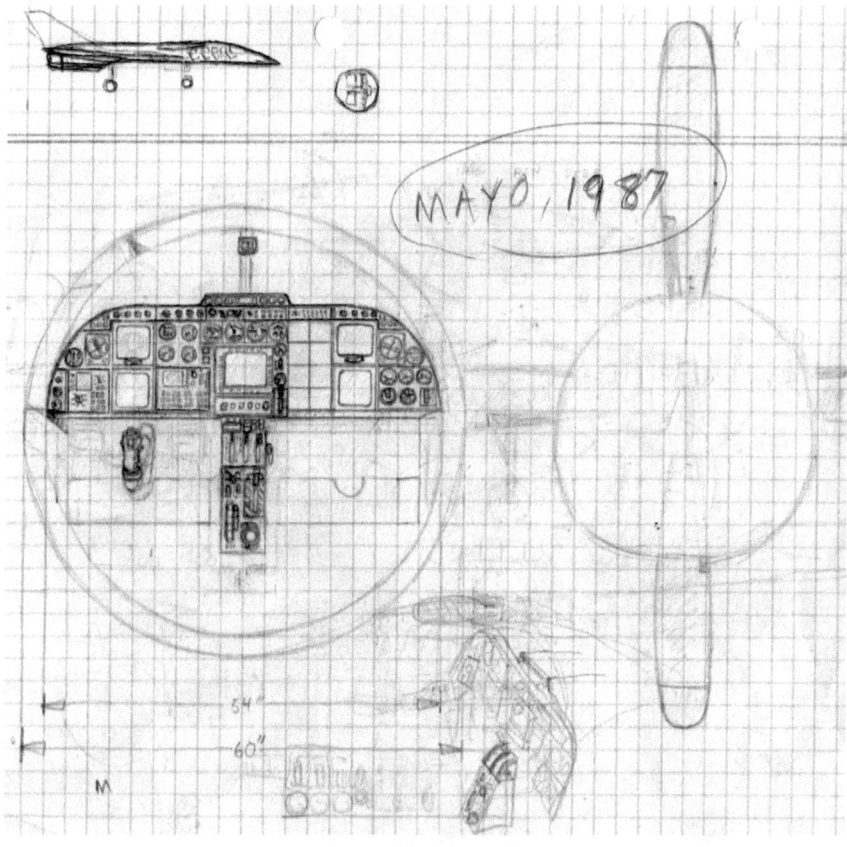

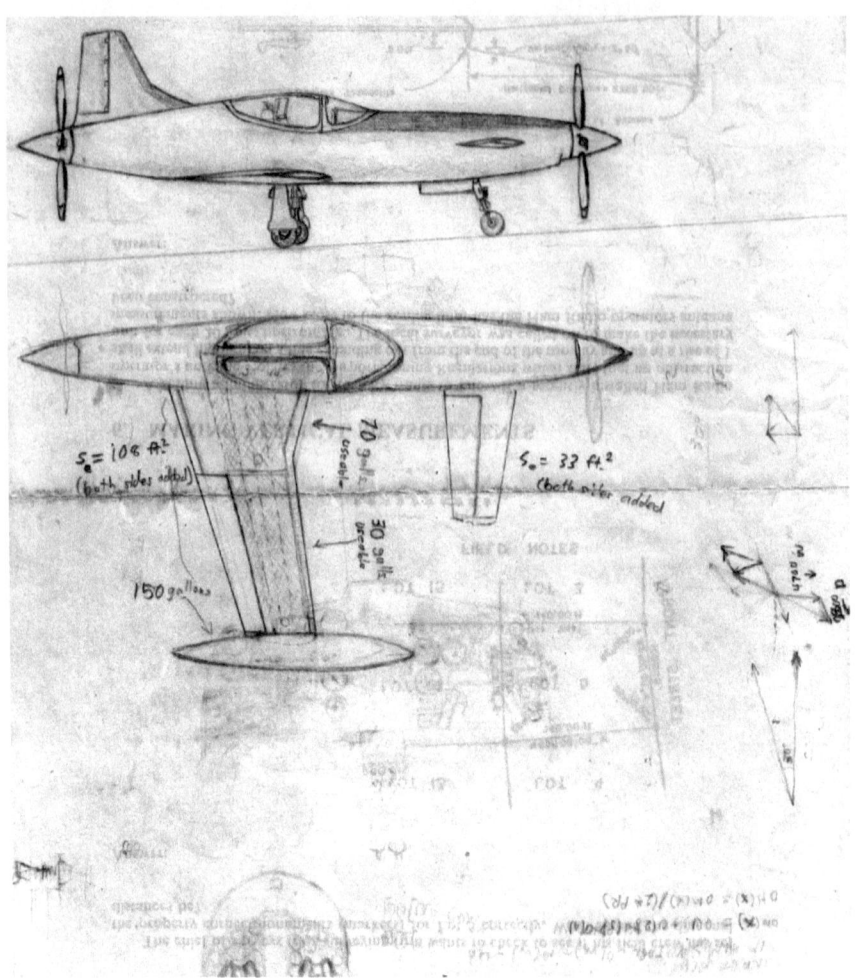

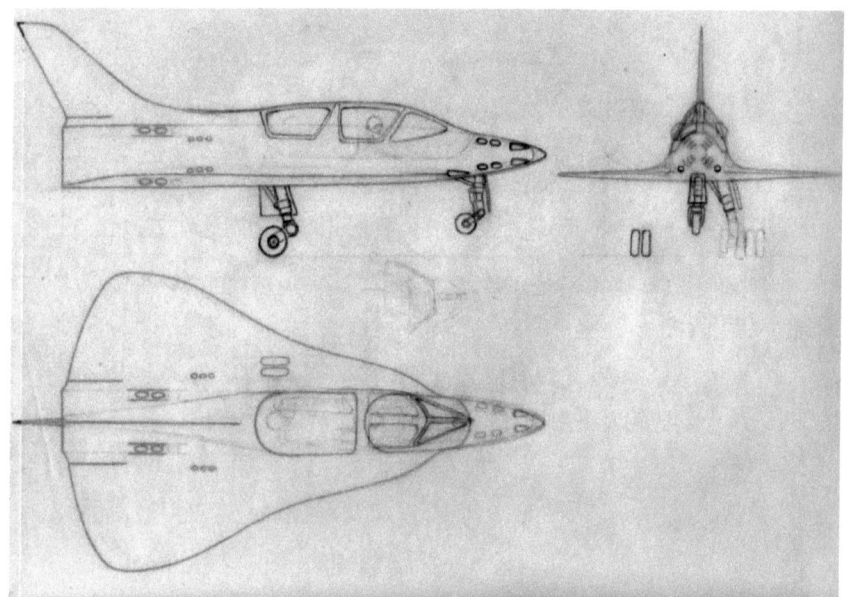

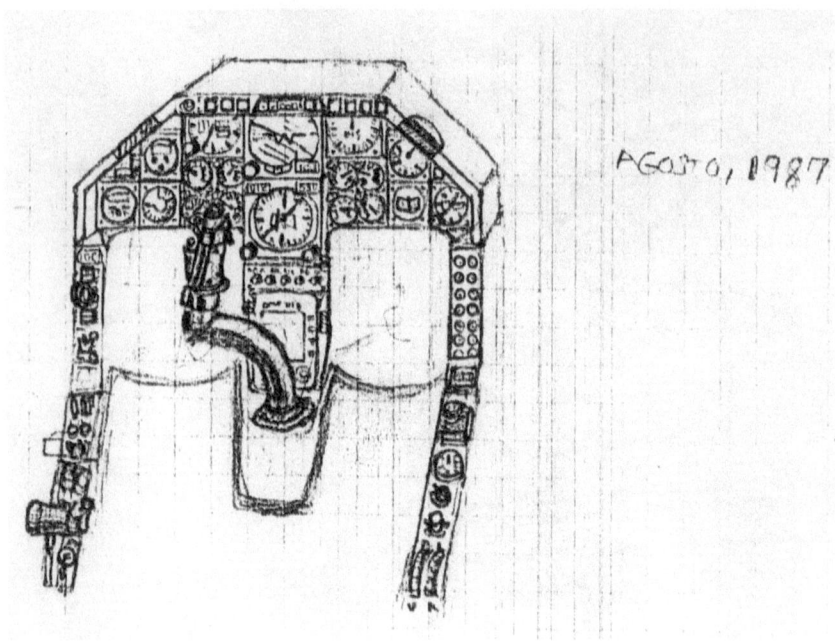

AGOSTO, 1987

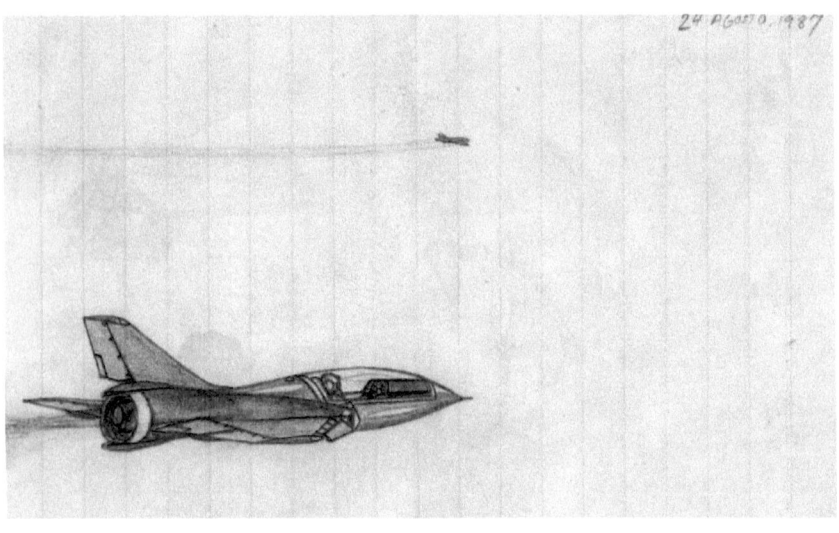

24 AGOSTO, 1987

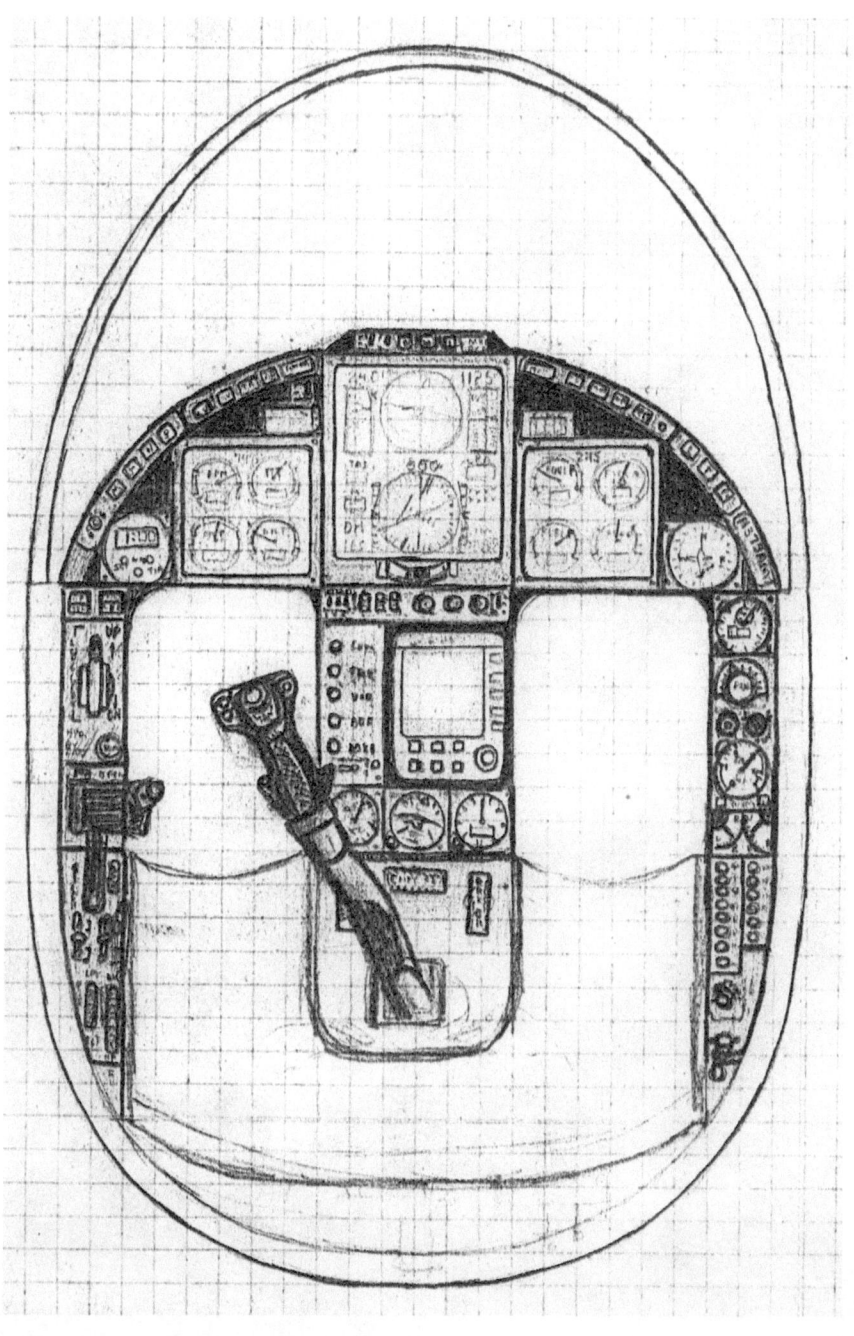

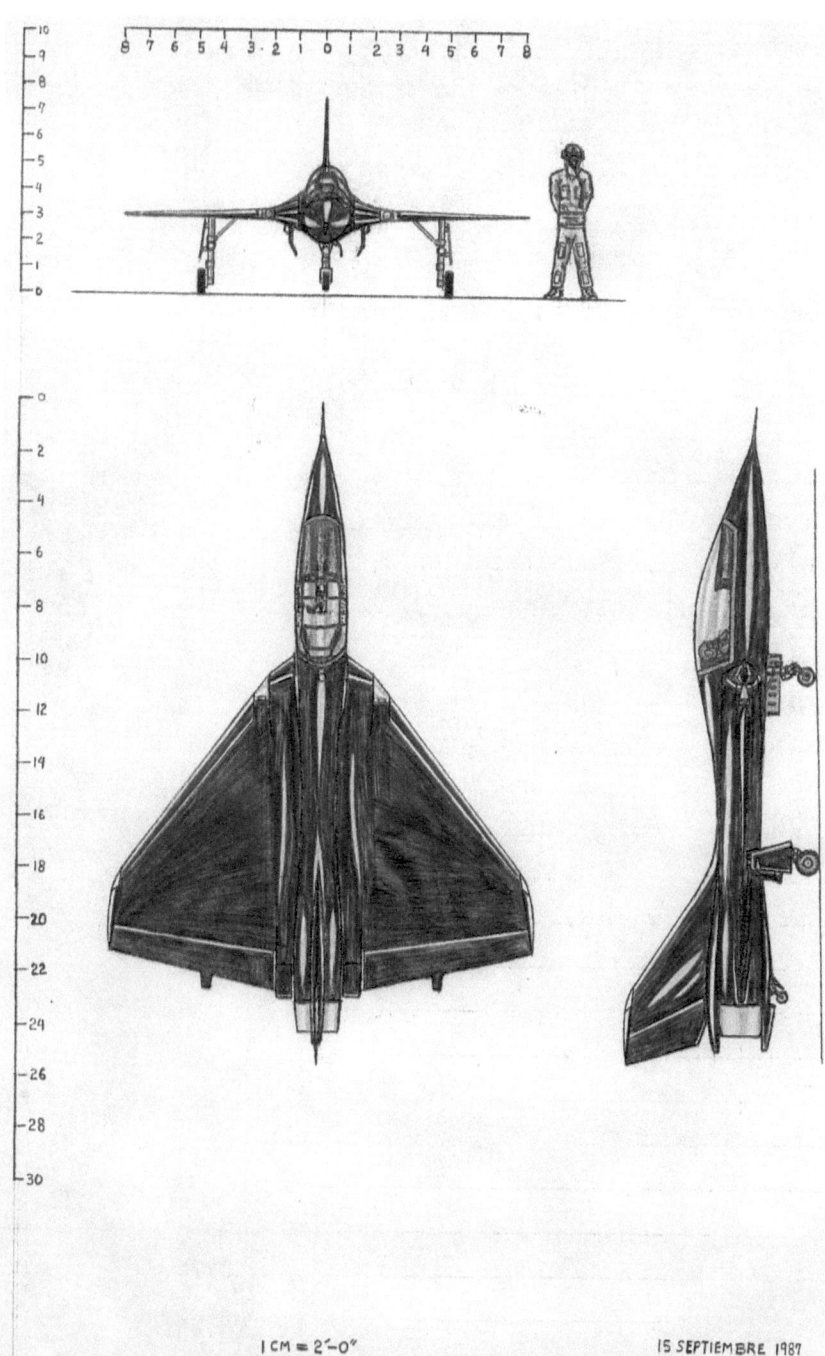

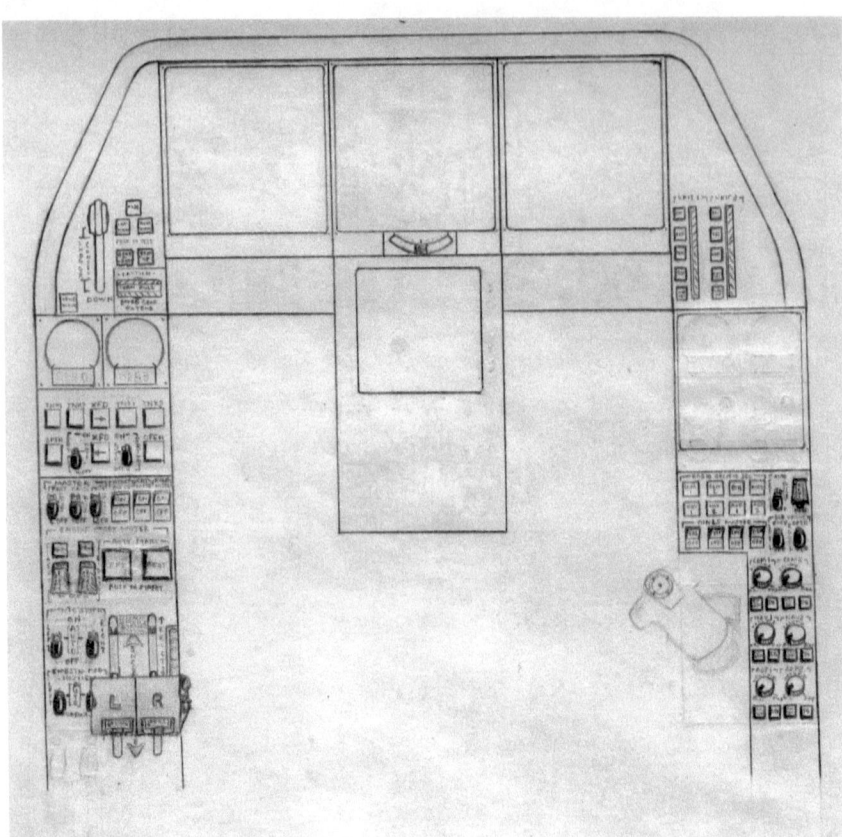

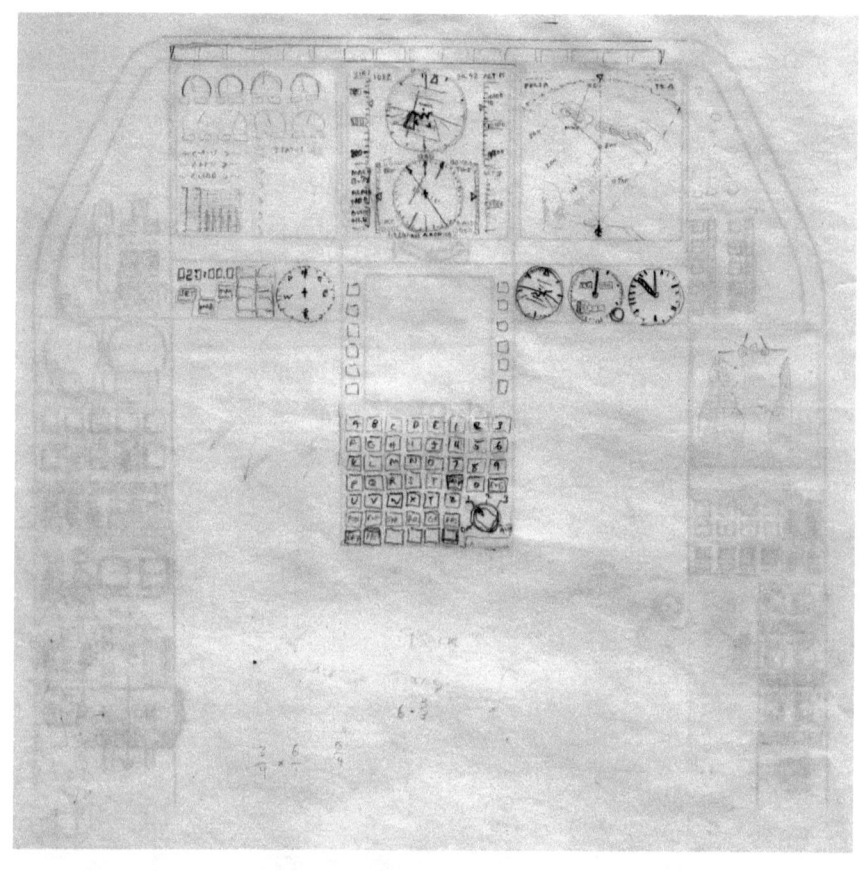

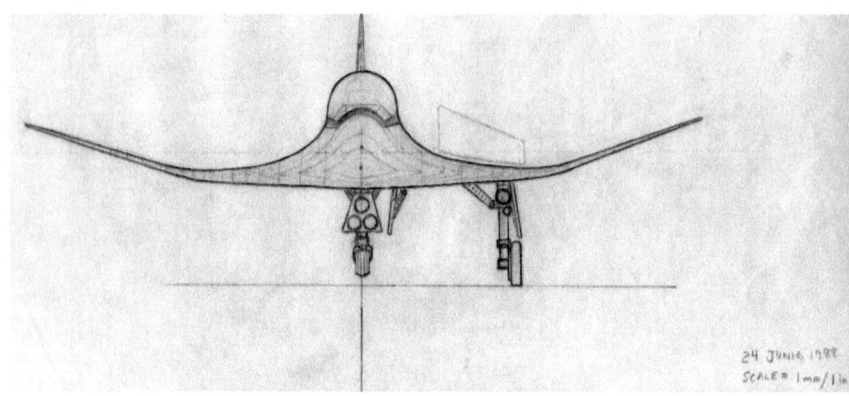

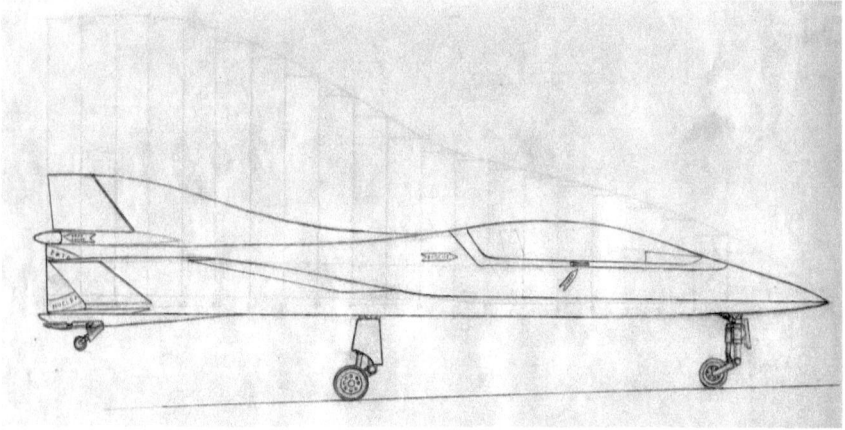

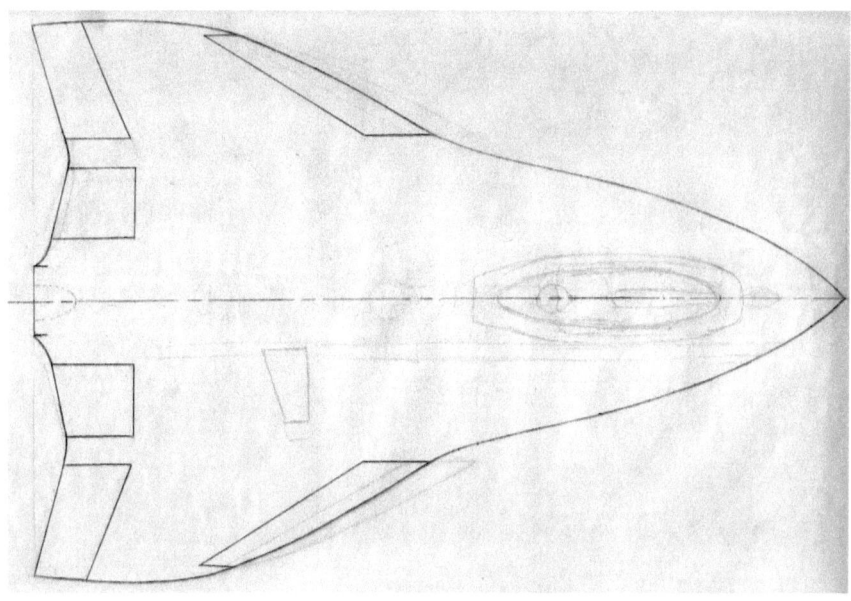

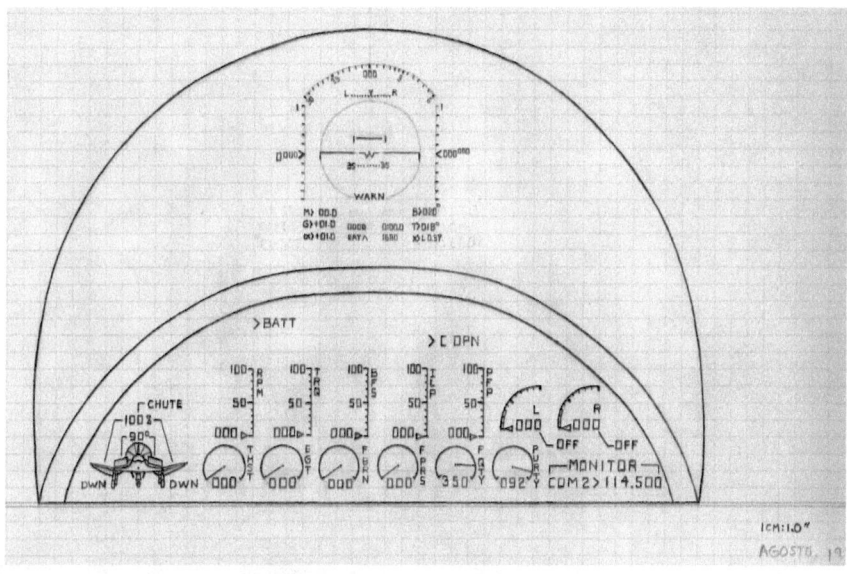

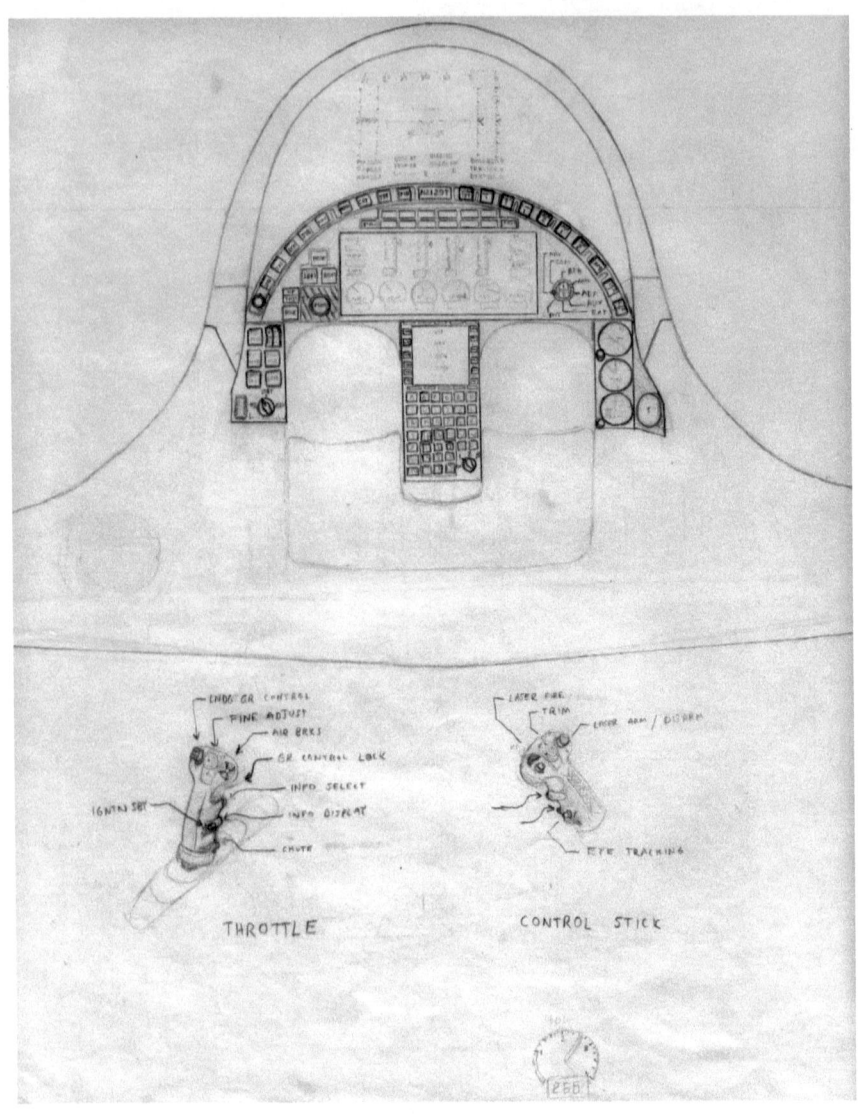

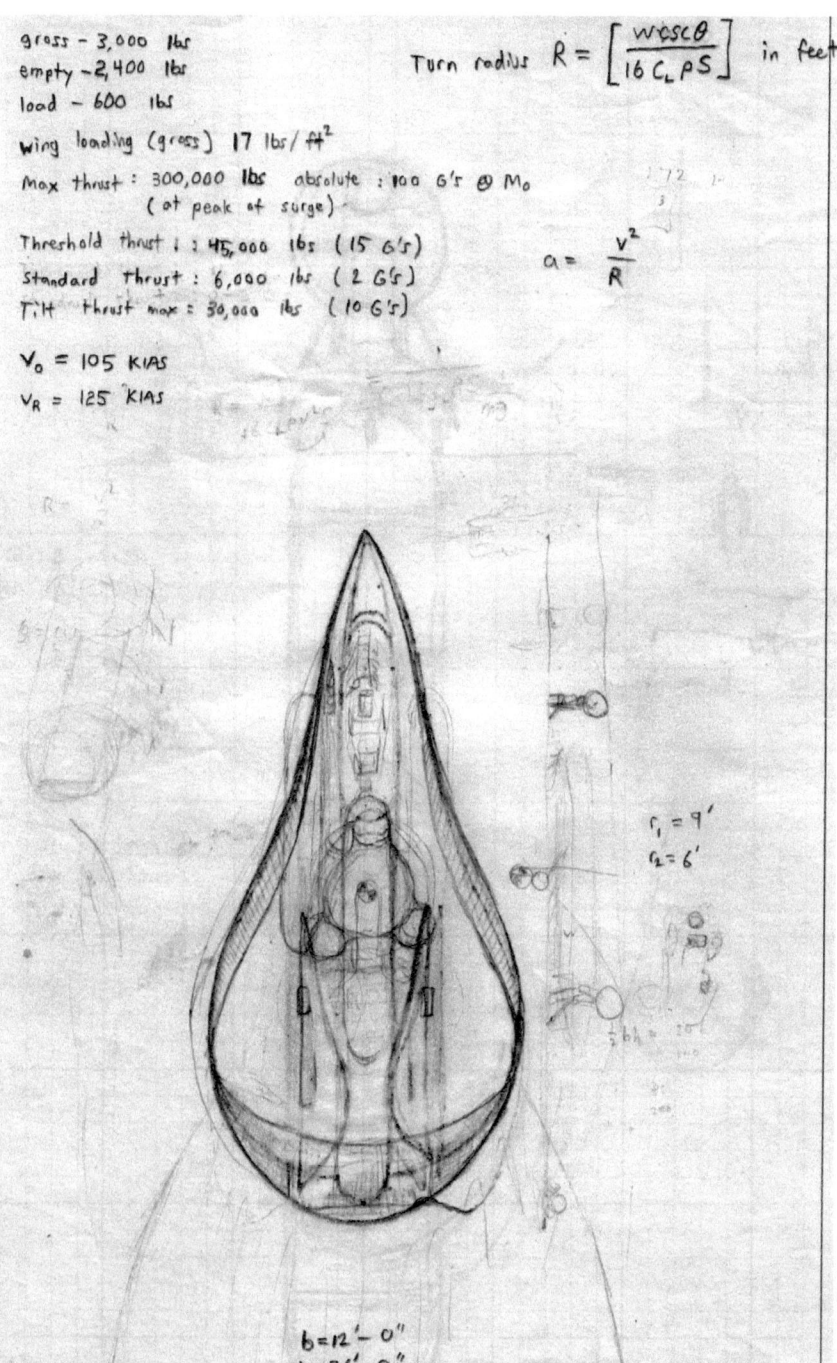

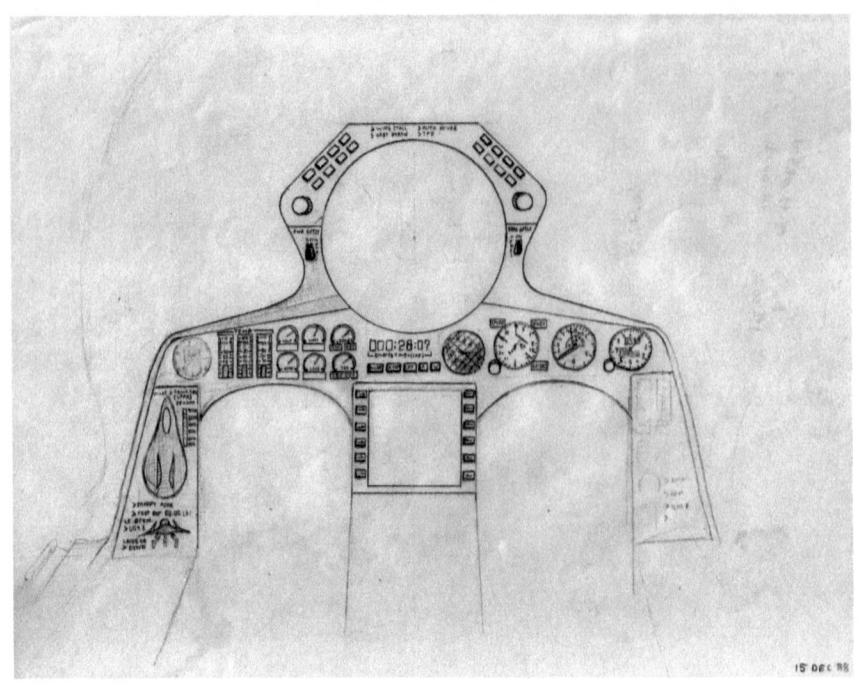

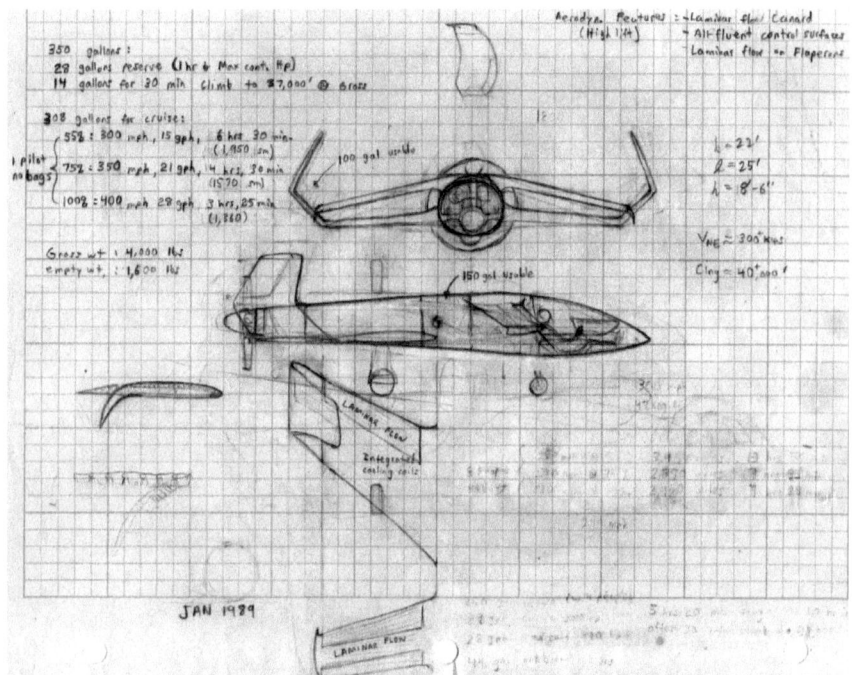

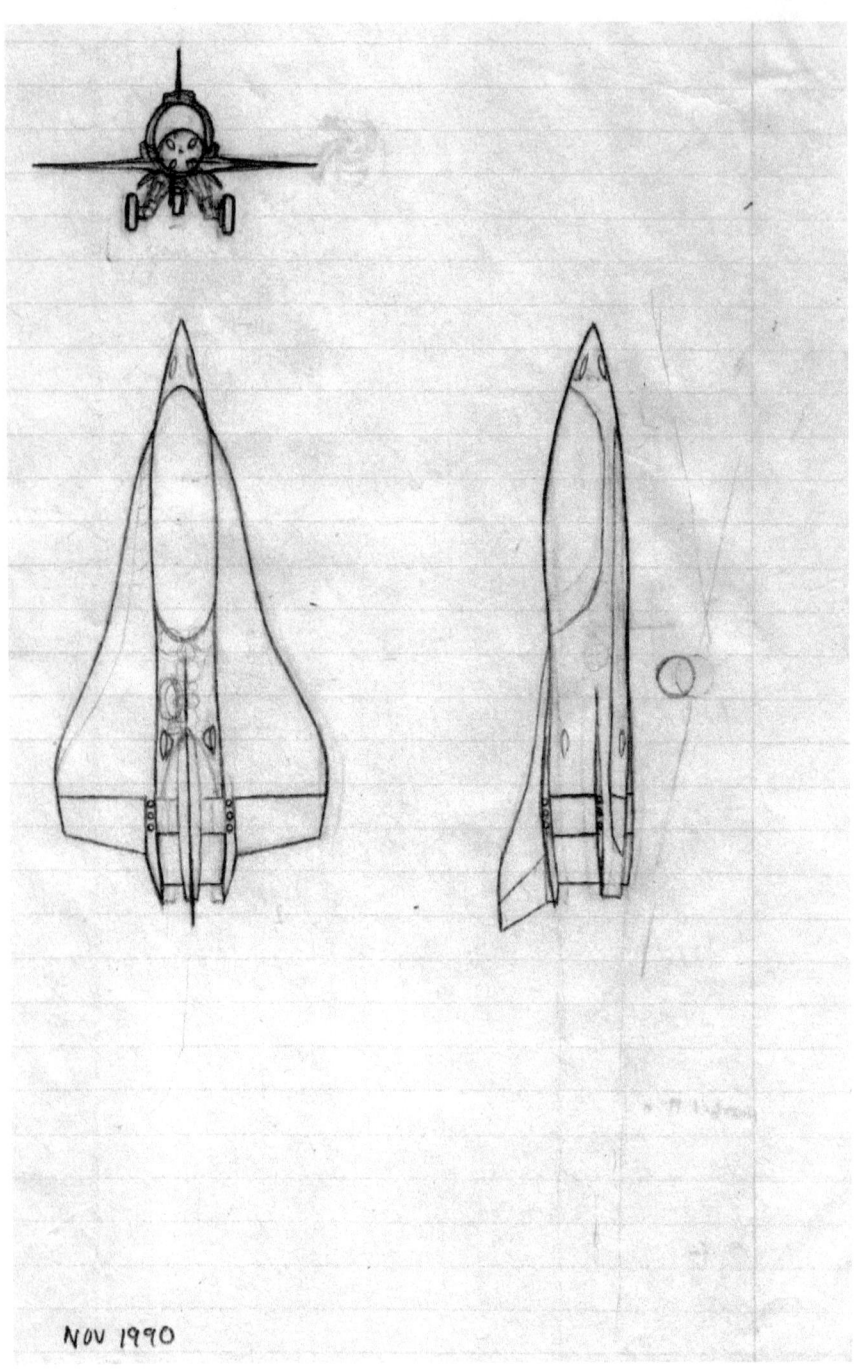

2 SCALE: 1 mm = 3 inches

DEC 1990

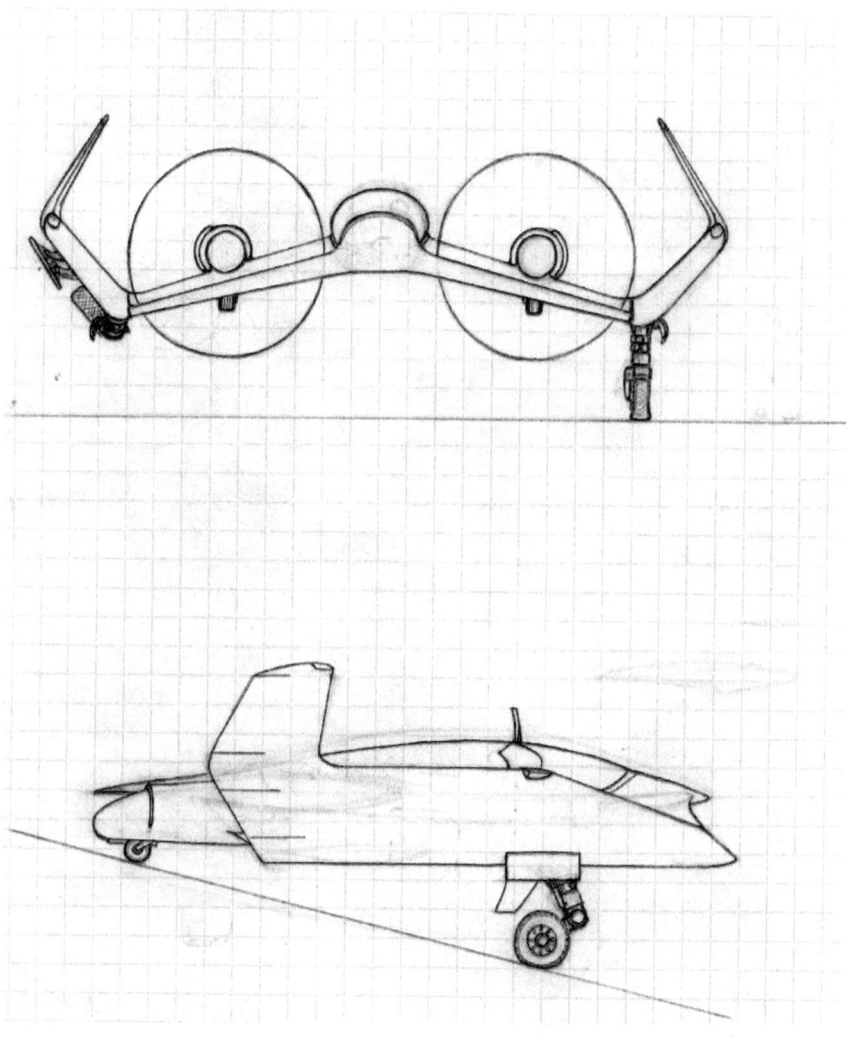

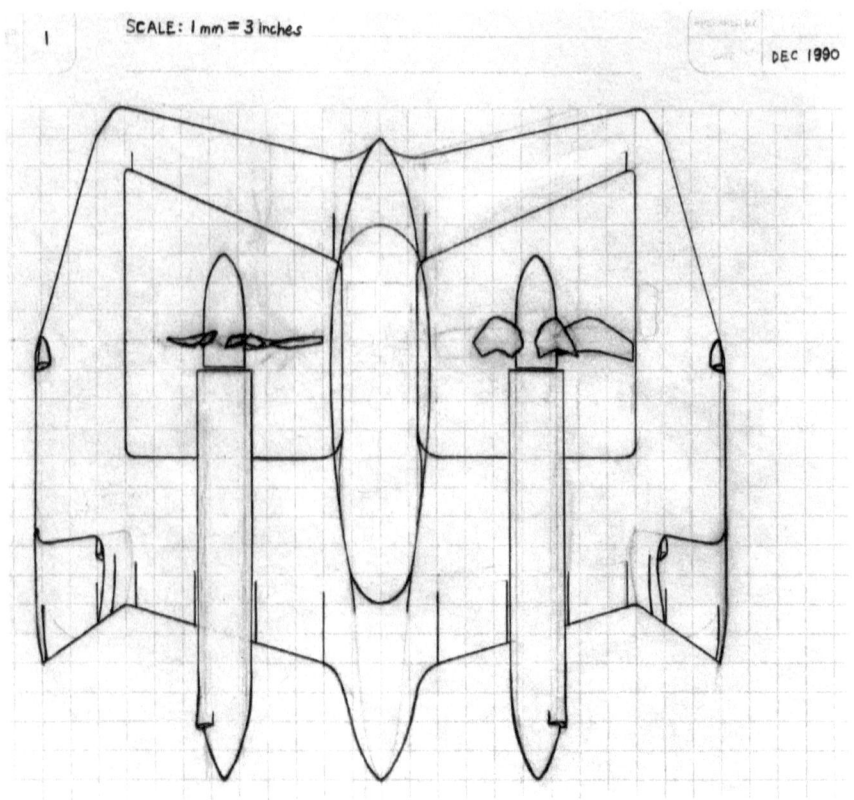

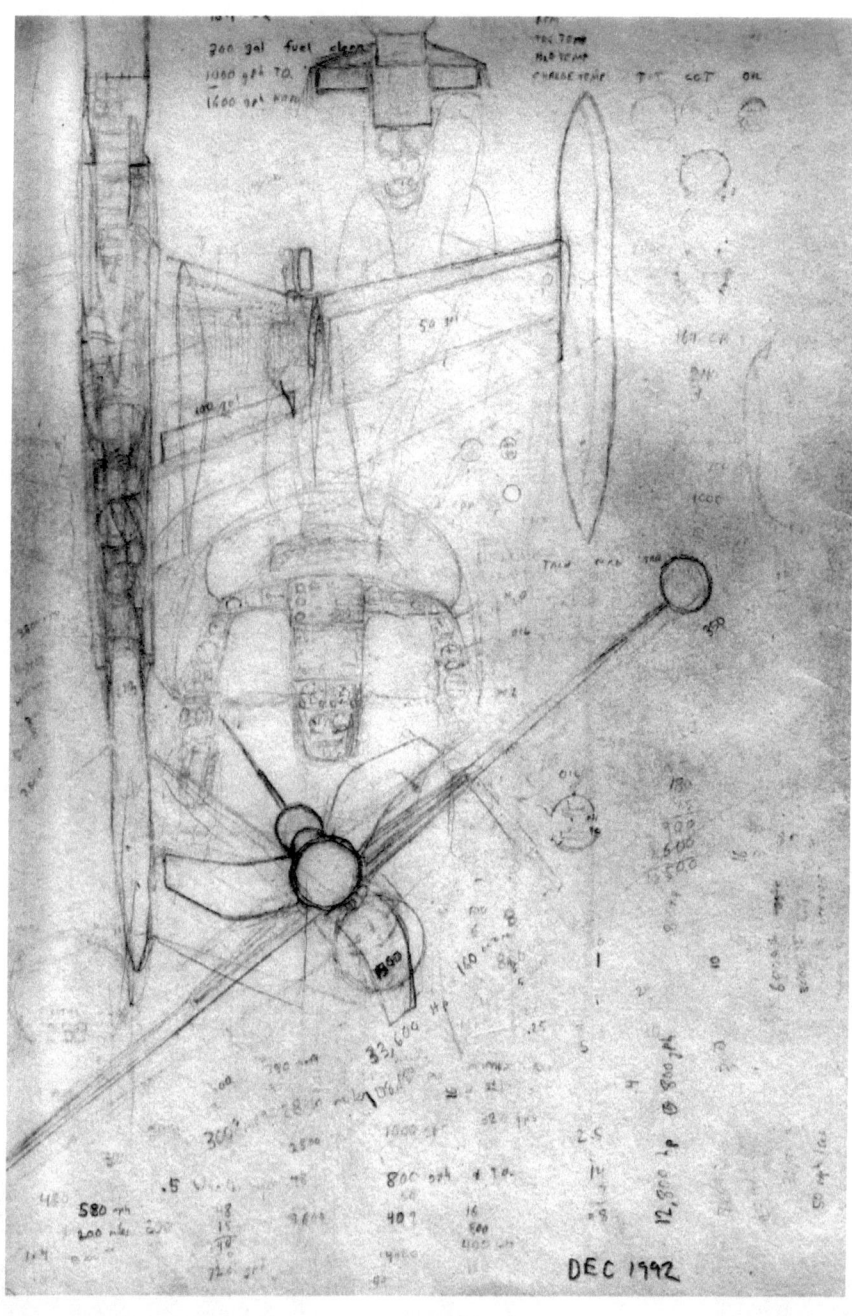

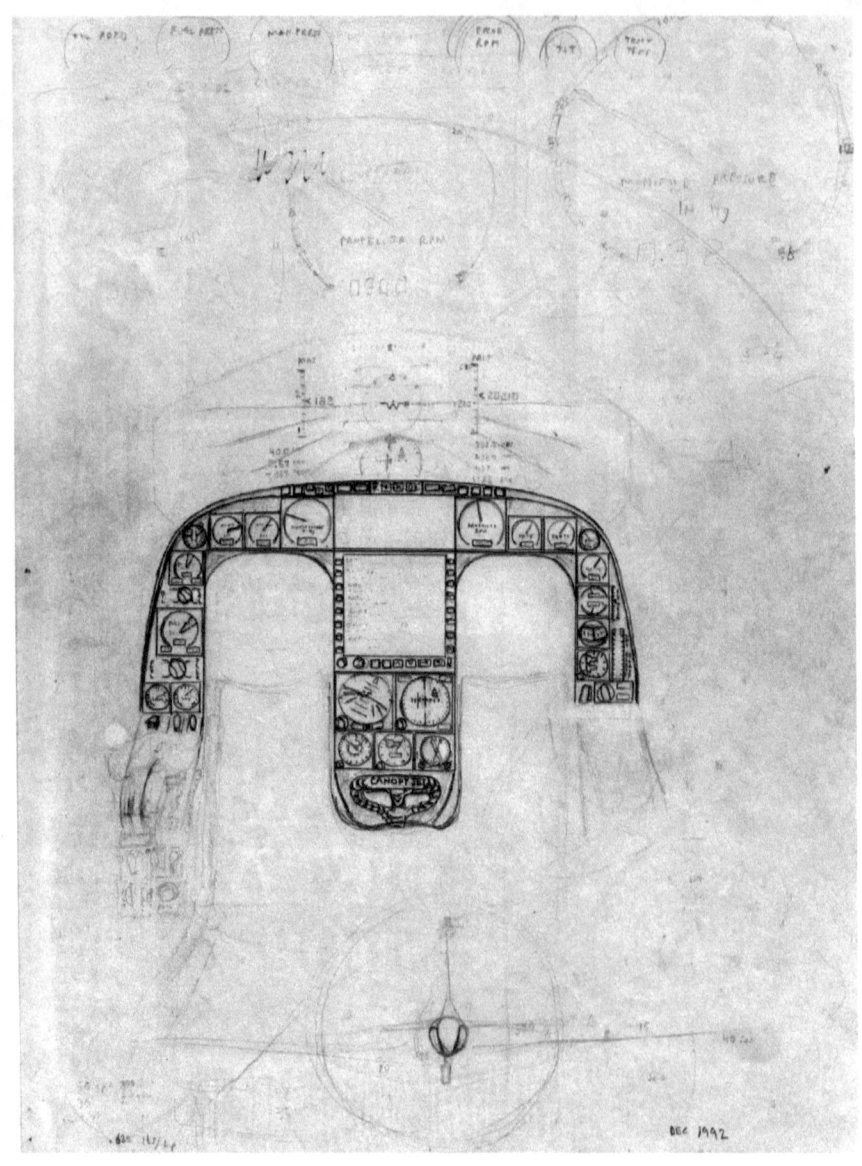

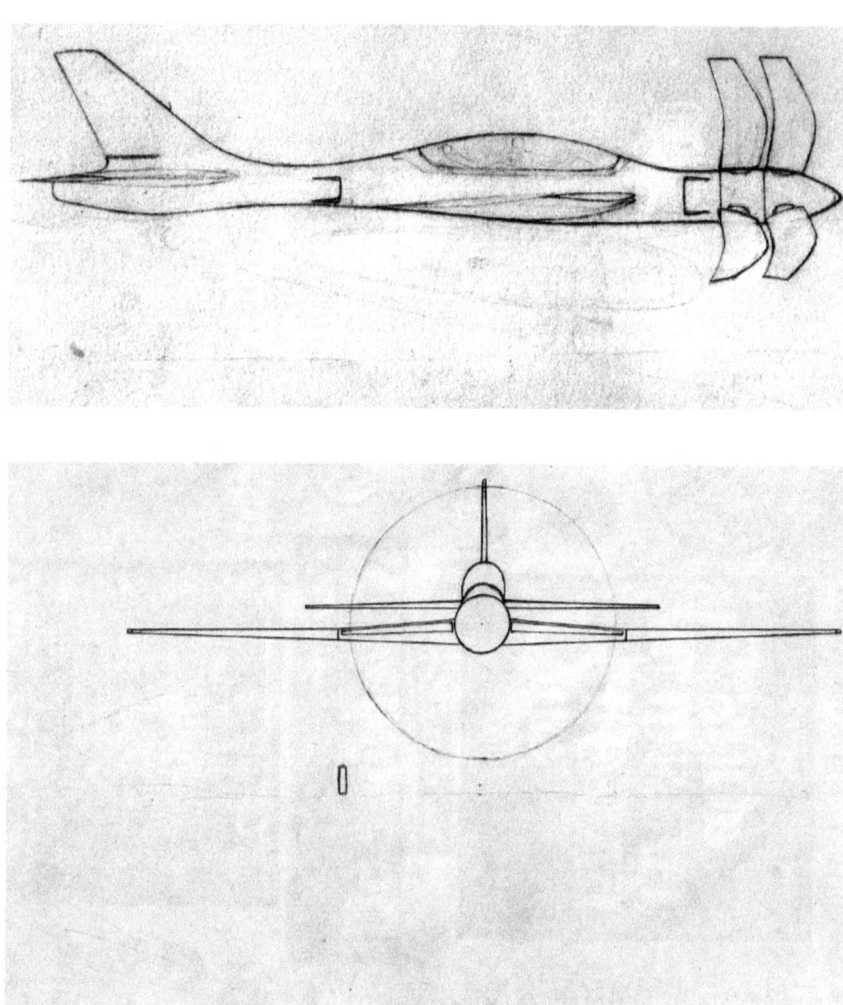

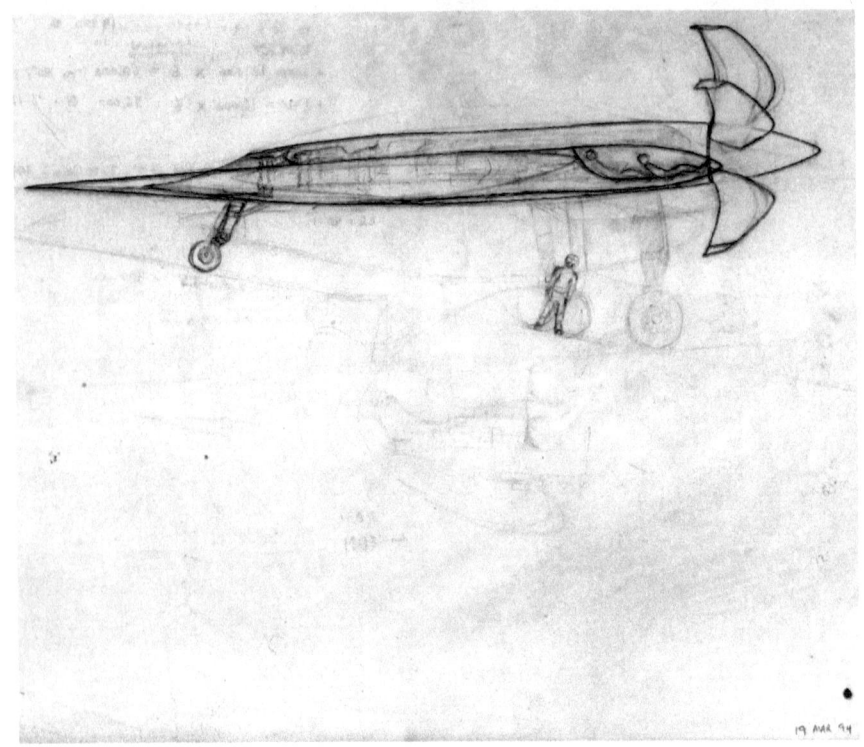

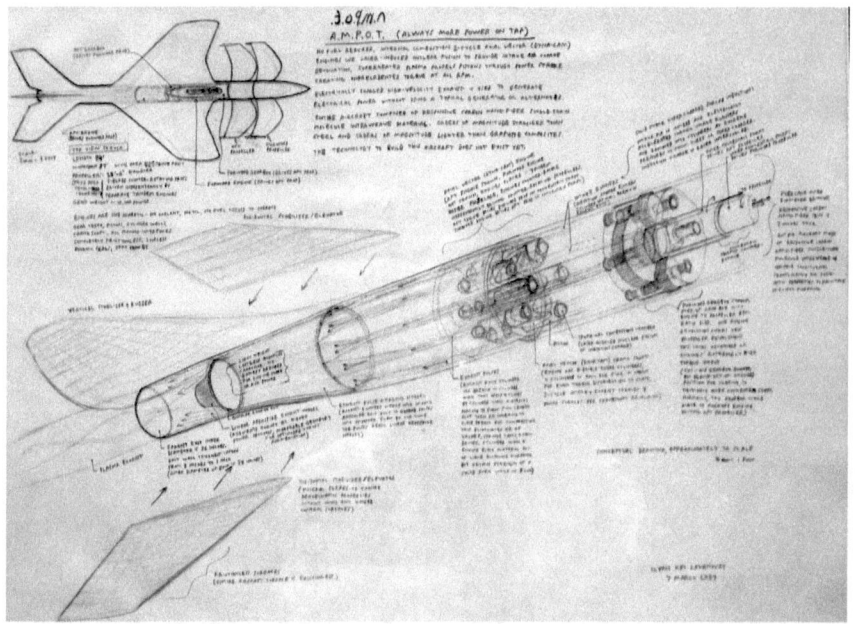

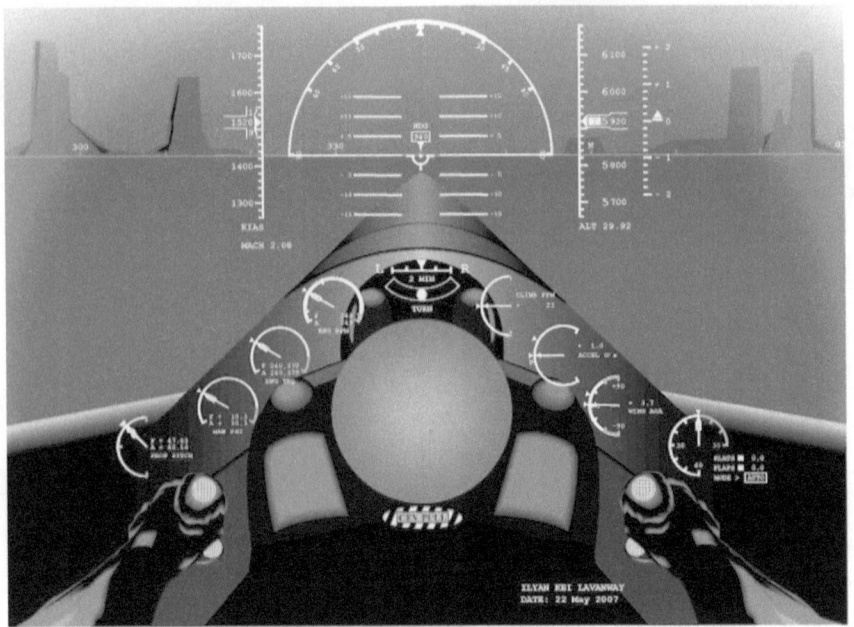

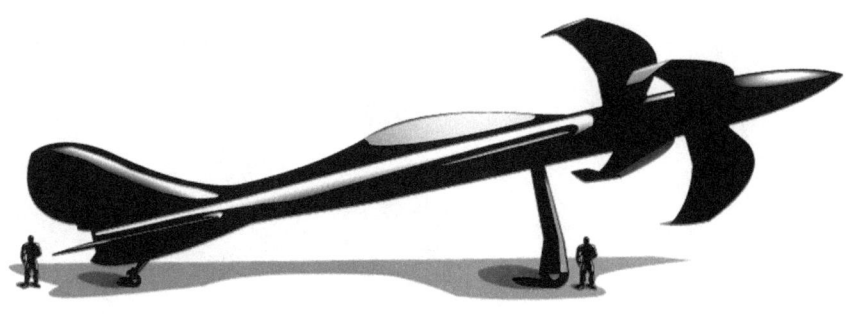

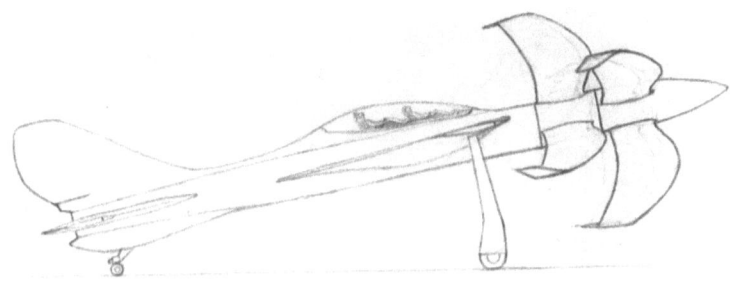

Photos

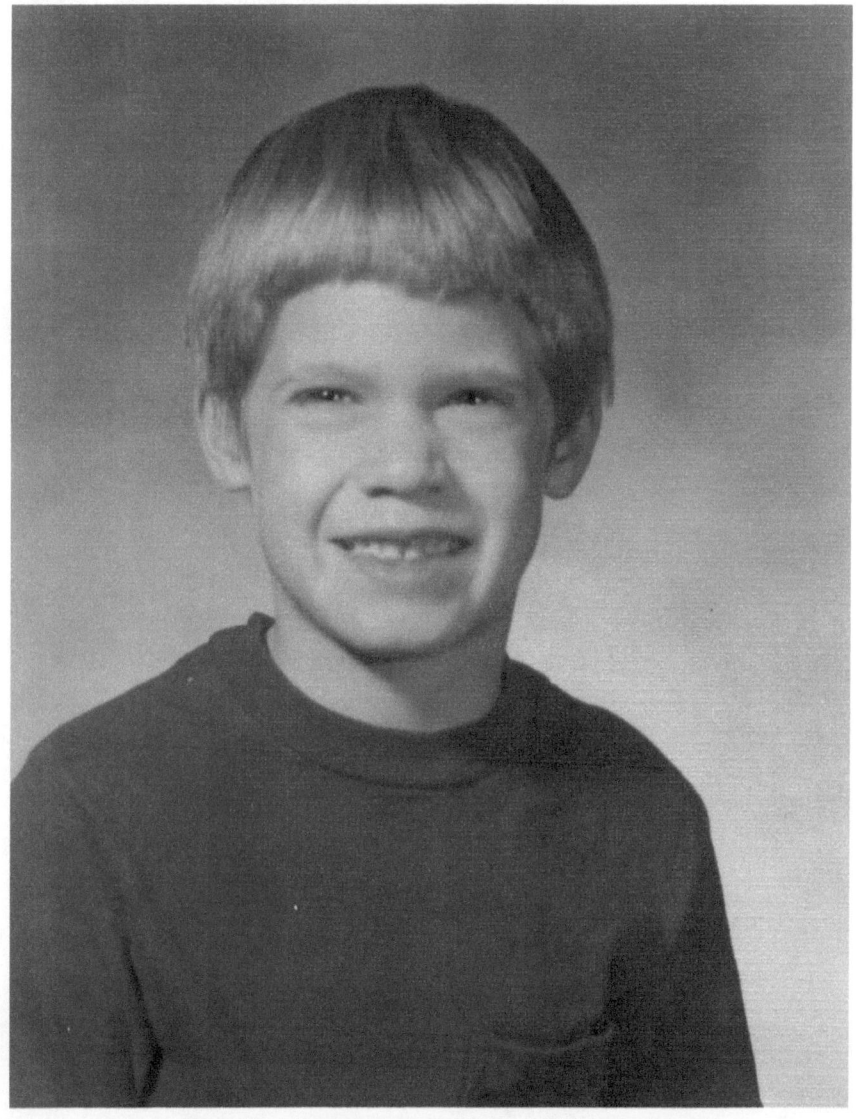

Ilyan Kei Lavanway, approximately age six.

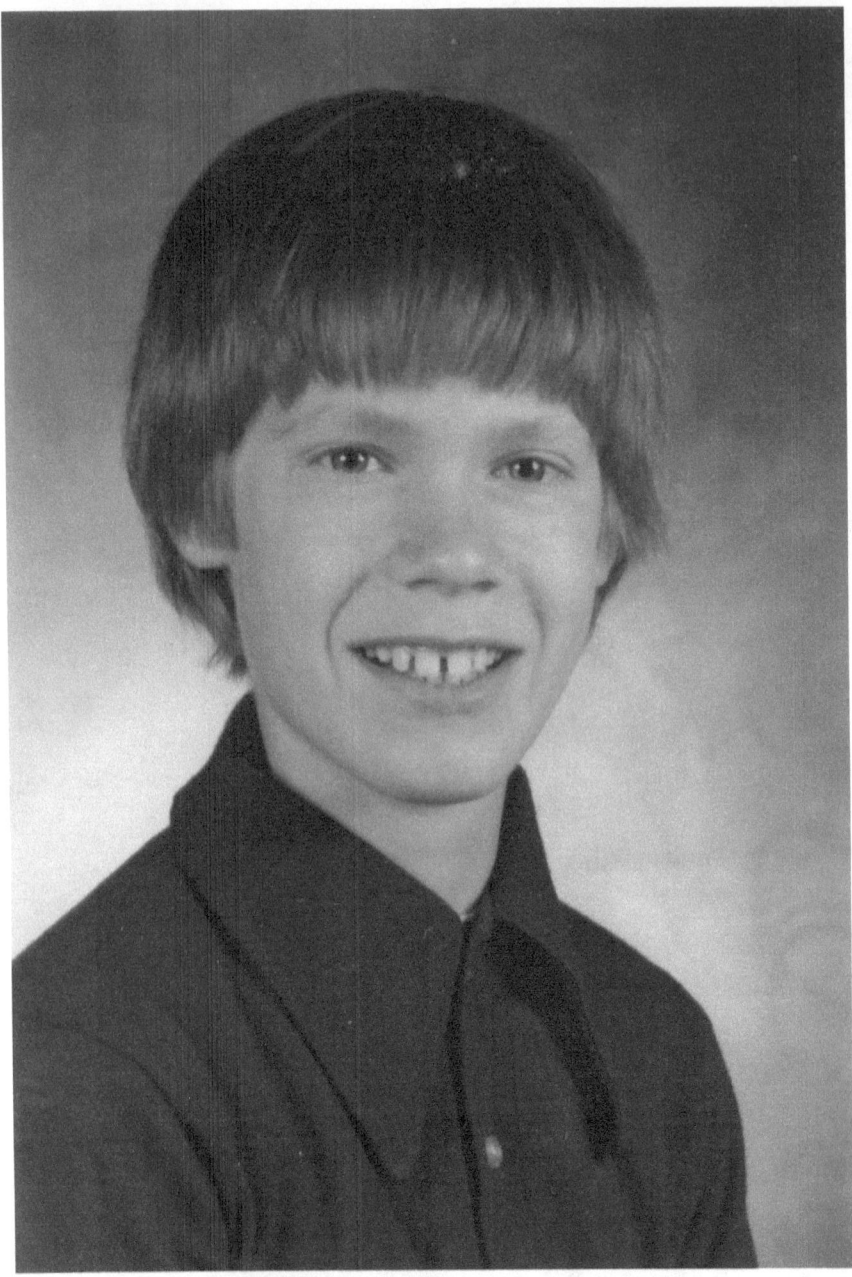

Ilyan Kei Lavanway, approximately age eight.

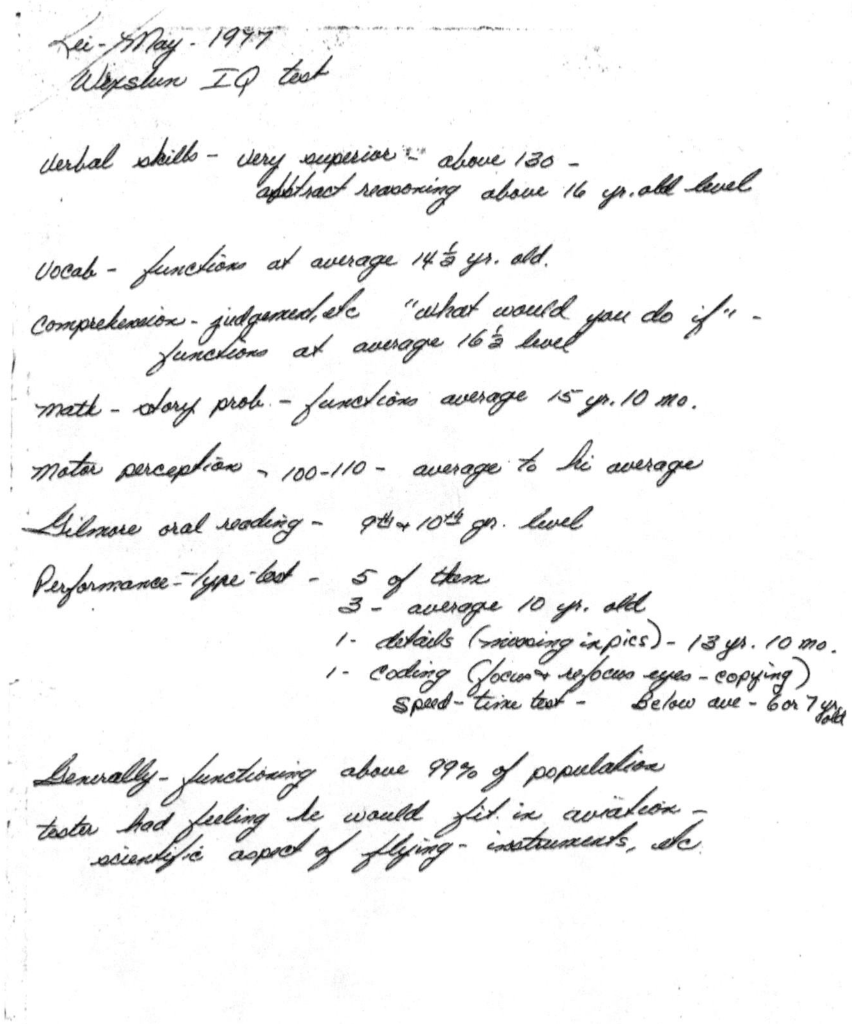

> Lei - May - 1977
> Wexslen IQ test
>
> verbal skills — very superior — above 130 —
>   abstract reasoning above 16 yr. old level
>
> Vocab — functions at average 14½ yr. old.
> Comprehension — judgement, etc "what would you do if" —
>   functions at average 16½ level
> math — story prob — functions average 15 yr. 10 mo.
> motor perception — 100-110 — average to hi average
> Gilmore oral reading — 9th & 10th gr. level
> Performance-type-test — 5 of them
>   3 — average 10 yr. old
>   1 — details (missing in pics) — 13 yr. 10 mo.
>   1 — coding (focus & refocus eyes — copying)
>   speed-time test — Below ave — 6 or 7 yrs old
>
> Generally — functioning above 99% of population
> tester had feeling he would fit in aviation —
>   scientific aspect of flying — instruments, etc

IQ test results, May 1977, age ten, noted in the handwriting of my mother, Genelle LaVanway.

UNITED STATES ACHIEVEMENT ACADEMY NATIONAL AWARDS 1981–1982

VOLUME VII
United States National Mathematics Awards

Copyright 1982
UNITED STATES ACHIEVEMENT ACADEMY
2570 Palumbo Drive
Lexington, Kentucky 40509

LAVANWAY, KEI; ALGEBRA I; ORCHARD JUNIOR HIGH SCHOOL; WENATCHEE; WA; Spon FLOYD CLINE; Boy Scts; Chrch Act; Explrng; Hnr Rol; Karate; Scout Act; Swim.

KEI LAVANWAY
ALGEBRA I
Orchard Junior High School
Wenatchee WA

Ilyan Kei Lavanway (left) with flight instructor, Jim Watson (right) on day of first solo flight, April 8, 1983, Cessna-152, N48868, Columbia Skyways, Pangborn Field, East Wenatchee, Washington.

Ilyan Kei Lavanway performing preflight inspection for first solo flight, April 8, 1983, Cessna-152, N48868, Columbia Skyways, Pangborn Field, East Wenatchee, Washington.

Ilyan Kei Lavanway, Eagle Scout, age seventeen, October 1984

Back from left: Brian Lewis, Ryan Moore, Stacy Hill, Ilyan Kei Lavanway
Front from left: Spencer White, Tom Manseau, Hunter Moses

Photo courtesy of The Wenatchee World, Thursday, October 4, 1984.

WHO'S WHO
AMONG AMERICAN
HIGH SCHOOL STUDENTS

1984-1985

Who's Who
Among American
High School Students®
Honoring Tomorrow's Leaders Today®

1984-85
Nineteenth Annual Edition
Volume X

WHO'S WHO AMONG AMERICAN HIGH SCHOOL STUDENTS® is a publication of Educational Communications, Inc. of Lake Forest, Illinois and has no connection with "Who's Who in America" and its publisher, Marquis — Who's Who, Inc. Students featured in this volume attended school in the following states: Alaska, California, Guam, Hawaii, Oregon and Washington.

Compilation of the copyright matter published in this volume has been accomplished only through the expenditure of considerable time, a monumental effort and at a great cost, and is intended for the exclusive use of our subscribers. Such information may not be key punched, entered into a computer or photocopied in any manner for any purpose whatsoever. Its use as a mailing list, either in whole or in part, is strictly forbidden. The contents have been coded and cannot be copied without detection; infringements will be prosecuted.

©Copyright 1985
Educational Communciations, Inc.
721 N. McKinley Road
Lake Forest, Illinois 60045
Printed in U.S.A.
ISBN 0-930315-11-1
ISBN 0-930315-01-4 (10 Volume Set)
Library of Congress Catalog Card Number 68-43796

WHO'S WHO AMONG AMERICAN HIGH SCHOOL STUDENTS® is a registered trademark owned by Educational Communications, Inc.

AY, ILYAN KEI; Waterville HS; Waterville, WA; (Y); 1/21; St; Boy Scts; Church Yth Grp; Scholastic Bowl; VP Sr Cls; b Sci Awd; NHS; CAP; Cmnty Wkr; Debate Tm; ROTC Air hp 85; Embry-Riddle Aeron U; Aeron Eng.

**Lavanway, Ilyan Kei
Waterville HS
Waterville, WA**

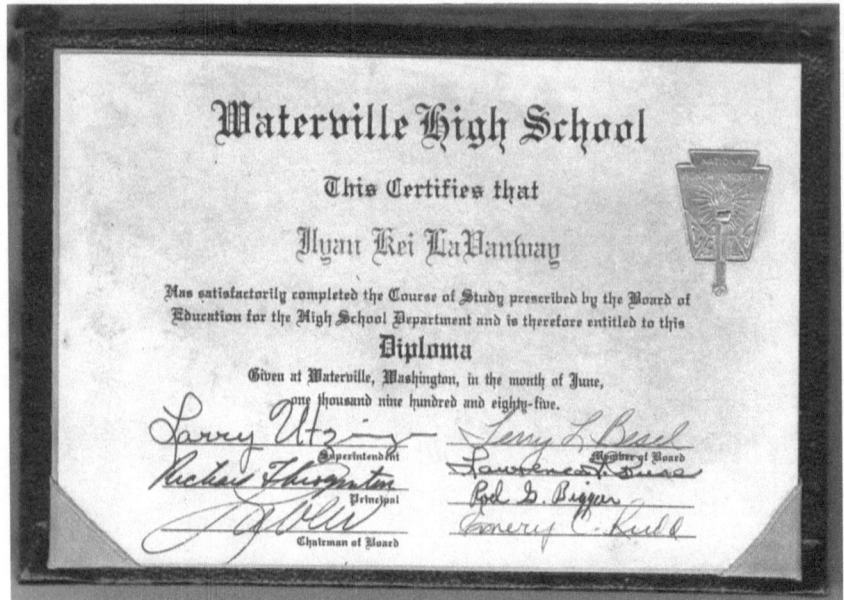

Ilyan Kei Lavanway, high school diploma, Waterville, Washington State, June 1985

LaVanway gets scholarship

Civil Air Patrol cadet Kei LaVanway has received a four-year ROTC scholarship to Embry Riddle Aeronautical University's western campus at Prescott, Ariz.

LaVanway is a senior at Waterville High School and is a flight officer in the local Civil Air Patrol squadron. His parents are Victor and Jeanelle LaVanway.

LaVanway is a licensed pilot and earlier received the Gen. Billy Mitchell award, a national Civil Air Patrol honor.

Ilyan Kei Lavanway with Mom, Genelle LaVanway, in back yard of home at 317 East Walnut Street, Waterville, Washington, on high school graduation day, June 1985.

Early January 1986. Piper PA-28R-200 Arrow, N2129T, in snow bank on northwest end of the taxiway at Waterville Airport, Washington State, after I hand propped the engine with no one manning the cockpit. I hand propped it because the starter Bendix gear would not engage. I am fortunate to be alive.

Ilyan Kei Lavanway, approximately age nineteen.

Ilyan Kei Lavanway, 1986, age nineteen, waiting at airport for a flight from California to Washington State.

Elder Ilyan Kei Lavanway, October 1986, Argentina Buenos Aires North Mission of The Church of Jesus Christ of Latter-day Saints. Photo with Mission President, Paul "Hap" Green and his wife.

Ilyan Kei Lavanway, approximately age twenty-two, about 1989.

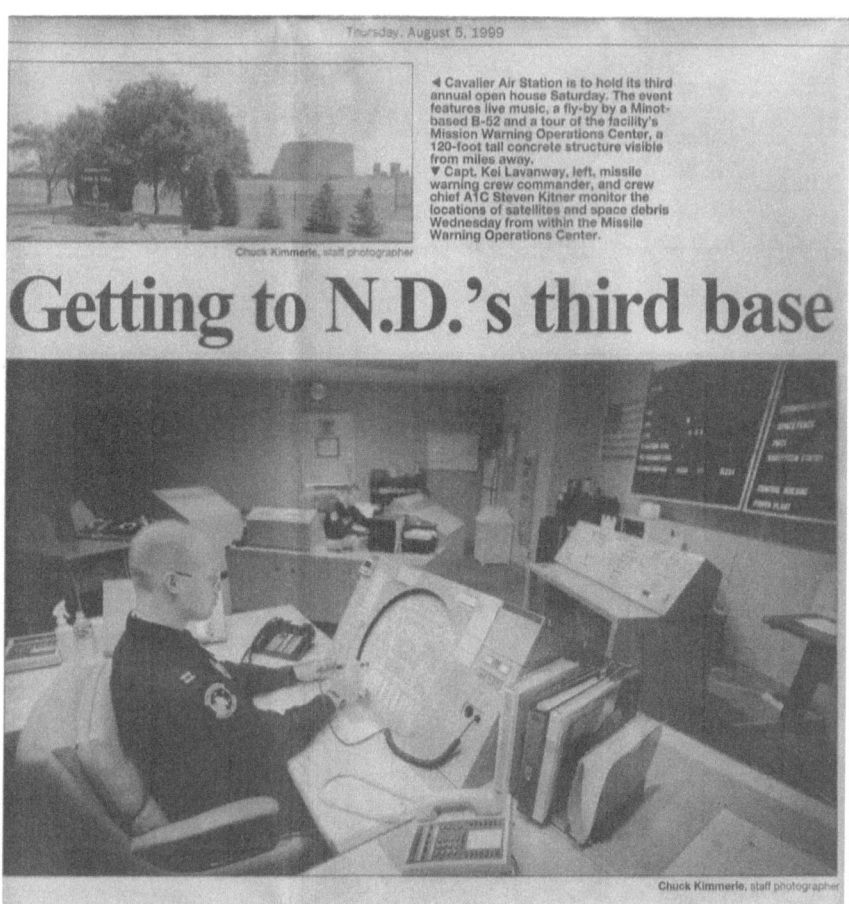

Captain Ilyan Kei Lavanway, Missile Warning Operations Center (MWOC), Cavalier Air Force Station, North Dakota, August 1999

Photo courtesy of Chuck Kimmerle, staff photographer, Grand Forks Herald, Thursday, August 5, 1999

Ilyan Kei Lavanway and Babygirl Menchie Javellana Lavanway, married April 3, 2000 in the Seattle Temple of The Church of Jesus Christ of Latter-day Saints. I still carry this photo in my wallet.

Ilyan Kei Lavanway and Babygirl Menchie Javellana Lavanway, Los Angeles, California Temple, April 4, 2001. This is not a wedding photo. We were married (sealed) in the Seattle Temple at sunrise, 0647 hours, April 3, 2000.

Ilyan Kei Lavanway and Buzz Aldrin, Vandenberg AFB, April 6, 2001

ILYAN KEI LAVANWAY

In 2002, while stationed at Los Angeles AFB, I tried to break into acting. Took some classes, got paid $50 as an extra in some cop show, and otherwise failed. But, I was the only guy who could start the cop car on set. I once owned a 1970 Chrysler Imperial that occasionally had to be started by crawling under the car and touching a screw driver between the starter and the chassis. This was the only technique that worked for the old cop car on the movie set.

Ilyan Kei Lavanway, 2002. No, I do not know how to ride a horse. The get-up just looked cool for a photo.

September 29, 2004, Mojave Airport, California. Second flight of privately developed rocket plane, SpaceShipOne, piloted by Mike Melville. Three months prior, SpaceShipOne became the world's first manned commercial space vehicle.

September 29, 2004. Ilyan Kei Lavanway (foreground) at Mojave Airport, California to watch second launch of SpaceShipOne piloted by civilian astronaut, Mike Melville.

Three months prior, on June 21, 2004, SpaceShipOne, built by Scaled Composites, became the first non-government, privately funded, manned spacecraft to officially achieve space flight, barely clearing the minimum required altitude of 62.14 miles. Civilian test pilot, Mike Melville became the first person to pilot a privately funded spacecraft into space.

Ilyan Kei Lavanway with one-month-old son, Immanuel Iron Lavanway, before sunrise, September 29, 2004, Mojave Airport, California. Aircraft designer, Burt Rutan's unique twin engine Boomerang aircraft is displayed in the background.

Other books:

Sevenfold (2013)

Intelligent Universe (2013)

Post Omerican Easter (2012)

The Modern Day Gadianton Golden Boy (2012)

Out of the Picture and Into the Picture (2012)

Platypus Boy on the Duck Farm (2012)

Duck Boy on the Platypus Farm (2012)

Earth Sink (2010)

Connect with me:

Email:
ilyanlavanway@yahoo.com

Amazon author page:
http://www.amazon.com/author/ilyan

Goodreads author page:
http://www.goodreads.com/ilyan

Smashwords author page:
https://www.smashwords.com/profile/view/ilyan

Self Publishers Showcase page:
http://selfpublishersshowcase.com/ilyan-kei-lavanway/

Facebook:
https://www.facebook.com/ConspiracyParanormal

LinkedIn:
http://www.linkedin.com/in/ilyanlavanway

Twitter:
https://twitter.com/ilyanlavanway

Blogs:
http://ebooksscifi.wordpress.com

http://conspiracyparanormal.blogspot.com

Websites:
http://ilyanlavanway.wix.com/books

http://conspiracyparanormal.com

www.ingramcontent.com/pod-product-compliance
Lightning Source LLC
Chambersburg PA
CBHW020945230426
43666CB00005B/171